Education in Drama:
Casting the Dramatic Curriculum

The Falmer Press Library on Aesthetic Education

Series Editor: Dr Peter Abbs, University of Sussex, UK

Setting the Frame

LIVING POWERS:
The Arts in Education
Edited by Peter Abbs

A IS FOR AESTHETIC:
Essays on Creative and Aesthetic
Education
Peter Abbs

THE SYMBOLIC ORDER:
A Contemporary Reader on the
Arts Debate
Edited by Peter Abbs

THE RATIONALITY OF
FEELING:
Understanding the Arts in
Education
David Best

The Individual Studies

FILM AND TELEVISION IN
EDUCATION:
An Aesthetic Approach to the
Moving Image
Robert Watson

LITERATURE AND
EDUCATION:
Encounter and Experience
Edwin Webb

THE VISUAL ARTS IN
EDUCATION
Rod Taylor

DANCE AS EDUCATION:
Towards a National Dance Culture
Peter Brinson

THE ARTS IN THE PRIMARY
SCHOOL
Glennis Andrews and Rod Taylor

MUSIC EDUCATION IN
THEORY AND PRACTICE
Charles Plummeridge

EDUCATION IN DRAMA:
Casting the Dramatic Curriculum
David Hornbrook

Work of Reference

KEY CONCEPTS:
A Guide to Aesthetics, Criticism and the Arts in Education
Trevor Pateman

Education in Drama:
Casting the Dramatic Curriculum

David Hornbrook

The Falmer Press

(A member of the Taylor & Francis Group)
London • New York • Philadelphia

UK   The Falmer Press, 4 John Street, London, WC1N 2ET

USA   The Falmer Press, Taylor & Francis Inc., 1900 Frost Road, Suite 101, Bristol, PA 19007

First published 1991   Reprinted 1993

British Library Cataloguing in Publication Data
Hornbrook, David
   Education in drama: Casting the dramatic curriculum.
   — (Falmer Press Library on aesthetic education)
   I. Title   II. Series
   792.07

   ISBN 1-85000-720-9
   ISBN 1-85000-721-7 pbk

**Library of Congress Cataloging-in-Publication Data
available on request**

Jacket design by Benedict Evans

Typeset in 12/14 pt Bembo
by Graphicraft Typesetters Ltd., Hong Kong

Printed in Great Britain by Burgess Science Press, Basingstoke on paper which has a specified pH value on final paper manufacture of not less than 7.5 and is therefore 'acid free'.

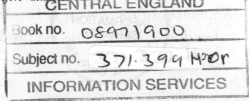

Contents

List of Figures

Acknowledgments

Thanks are due to Cary Bazalgette and the British Film Institute for permission to reprint 'Signpost Questions' from *Primary Media Education*, to Longman for the extract from *The Arts 5–16* and to HMSO for the Levels of Attainment diagram from the TGAT Report.

My personal thanks go to those friends and colleagues who painstakingly helped with early drafts of this book and who spotted the worst of my gaffes. Peter Abbs, Alistair Black, Sian Ede, Fred Inglis, Eileen McAndrew and Cecily O'Neill in particular lent their experience and judgment to my project and I am greatly indebted to them.

David Hornbrook
London
February 1991

Series Editor's Preface

In *Living Powers* (1987), the first volume of the Aesthetic Library, Christopher Havell in his study of drama in the curriculum concluded:

> The rift between drama and theatre has been so deep and the divorce from tradition so complete that it may take another decade before teachers can comfortably draw upon the past as a source of guidance about their craft.[1]

Three years later it might be justly asserted that the author's insight was sound but that his prediction was far too pessimistic. For during the last few years the remarkable success of Theatre Studies at 'A' and GCSE levels indicates a growing fusion of drama and theatre and now, in this volume, David Hornbrook presents a programme of artistic work for teachers, which, to use his own words, stretches from ancient times to the dramas of the students' own experiences. The revolution in drama, for such it is, is taking place with an astonishing speed and force even if the context for its development remains precarious. Before our eyes, drama is reconstituting itself as a coherent arts discipline within the generic community of the arts.

Yet the position developed in this book remains controversial and many drama teachers will feel somewhat insecure before its demands. It is not difficult to understand the nature of that unease if we briefly consider the recent tradition of drama teaching in this country. As David Hornbrook suggests in this study (and argues more fully elsewhere),[2] the dominant, if not exclusive, approach to drama for the last forty years has been child-centred and psychological in its orientation, not aesthetic. The titles alone of two key books — Peter Slade's *Child Drama* (1954) and Brian Way's *Development through Drama* (1967) — display well enough the central unifying preoccupations. Such preoccupations with the child and its psychological state radically cut short any notion of drama as the gradual initiation of the child into the variegated world of the theatre or, more broadly, into any collective aesthetic or historical dimension. In *Development through Drama* it was categorically stated: 'We are concerned with developing people not drama (and certainly not theatre)'.[3] In the 1970s and 1980s drama changed again and the conception of 'drama as a learning medium' became, largely through the energetic work of Dorothy Heathcote and Gavin Bolton, hugely popular. But once again the new developments excluded any significant reference to actors, theatre and plays — what, in this study, David Hornbrook names the three conceptual outcasts. Drama was converted into an effective tool for enquiry which could be extended across the curriculum but, cut off from the aesthetic field, it forfeited any sense of intrinsic identity. Devoid of art, devoid of the practices of theatre, devoid of artistic and critical terminology drama became a method of teaching *without a subject*.

Again, in this context, it has to be said that the profound anti-intellectualism of the progressive movement within which, during the 1950s and 1960s, educational drama developed, failed inevitably to provide the necessary conceptual equipment. The whole movement celebrating 'self-expression', came to rely much too heavily on a tiny handful of charismatic gurus. I remember a well-known drama teacher saying to me with dogmatic passion: 'I *never* recommend a book', as if ideas were somehow inherently corrupting. As a result of such intellectual poverty there was never sufficient concern to establish, in the context of intellectual debate, those comprehensive structural principles which can identify the nature and extent of the discipline. For four decades the practice of drama seemed to rest on a number of simple and falsifying dichotomies — drama versus

theatre, process versus performance, the child versus the inherited culture, the open space versus the stage space — dichotomies which only required for their resolution a critical
broadening of categories.

The historical background helps to explain why some
drama teachers may be at first uneasy before the prospect of a
more integrated and comprehensive programme of artistic work
intellectually grounded in aesthetic and cultural principles. And
yet the sharp argument made in this book is not only long
overdue in the world of educational drama, it is also structurally
in accord with developments now taking place across all the arts
(especially in dance and the visual arts) and in the curriculum as
a whole. The re-envisaging of drama as an arts discipline within
the generic community of the arts is of the moment and now
has to be attended to in the open arena of educational debate.

Essentially what David Hornbrook offers in this book is an
organized framework for the development of drama for the
1990s. He is committed to a form of drama teaching which
develops designers, directors, performers, playwrights and critics, or, more accurately, which develops in children the activities of designing, directing, acting, writing and evaluating, all
within the great historic continuum of dramatic work. Through
a structuralist analysis of types of narrative — what he desig-
nates as the stage-text, the electronic-text and the social-text —
he is able to demarcate the field of drama and, in doing so, to
expand its range enormously. The analysis discloses fresh possibilities for drama, as well as a distinctive content, and reveals
simultaneously the paucity of much current practice based on an
exclusive diet of social themes and small or large group work.
Furthermore, David Hornbrook shows how the variegated
work based on types of dramatic narrative can be artistically
developed through a model similar to one outlined earlier in
Living Powers, namely by examining the activity through the
twin categories of *production* ('making' and 'presenting' in *Living
Powers*) and *reception* ('responding' and 'evaluating').[4] One won-
ders indeed, in this context, whether drama teachers haven't
much to learn from the growth of critical studies in the teaching
of the visual arts.[5] Finally, David Hornbrook, in the closing
chapter of the book, demonstrates that all the work proposed

for the drama programme can be convincingly assessed at the various stages and levels defined by the national curriculum. In short, drama is shown to be a distinctive subject which should be formally offered in any curriculum claiming balance and coherence.

Some readers may feel initially that the programme of work outlined here must return the teacher to the old mechanical methods of teaching, of say, reading the text round the class. Nothing could be further from the truth. All the classroom examples described and evoked by David Hornbrook show a dynamic method of work, with children wholly engaged in the aesthetic process of making, performing and responding. Not only that, but the model formally proposed, with certain qualifications, for the drama classroom is that of the 'dramatic laboratory' deriving from the Polish director, Jerzy Grotowski. Such an experimental forum cannot be more challenging as it is built on the principles of vulnerable experience and active exploration. The difference between the old drama and the new does not lie in method but *in content*, in the drawing in of a whole new range of works and techniques. It is a revolution in mapping, not style.

In brief the time has come for drama to reclaim its rightful artistic territory of theatre and text and to enter unequivocally into the generic community of the arts. In this book David Hornbrook provides not only the necessary signposts but a challenging framework for the changes.

Peter Abbs
Centre for Language, Literature and the Arts in Education
University of Sussex
September 1990

Notes and References

1   Havell, C. (1987) 'The case for drama', in Abbs, P. (Ed.) *Living Powers: the Arts in Education*, London, Falmer Press, ch. 6.

2 See Hornbrook, D. (1989) *Education and Dramatic Art*, Oxford, Basil Blackwell.
3 Way, B. (1967) *Development through Drama*, London, Longman.
4 *Living Powers*, pp. 56–62.
5 Taylor, R. (1986) *Educating for Art*, London, Longman.

Chapter 1

Setting the Stage

> Drama in schools is a practical artistic subject. It ranges
> from children's structured play, through classroom im-
> provizations and performances of specially devised mate-
> rial to performances of Shakespeare.
>
> HMI, 1989[1]

Actors, Theatres and Plays

It becomes increasingly clear that the incorporation of drama-
in-education within English in the national curriculum poses
a threat to the disciplinary independence of drama in schools in
England and Wales. While primary drama specialists may be
pleased that the statutory arrangements for English ensure role-
play and improvization a place under 'speaking and listening',
few, I suspect, are happy with the way the 1988 Education Act
effectively split the arts into national curriculum (visual art and
music) and non-national curriculum (dance and drama).[2] In
secondary schools there is a real danger that small but hard-
fought-for drama departments will be colonized by their English
neighbours, while lecturers on the few remaining initial teacher
training courses in drama may well speculate on how long it
will be before they become reduced to teaching options within
English majors.

As a response to a situation in which there is a real danger that drama could slip quietly from the curricula of our schools altogether, this book challenges the idea that drama is best thought of as part of English and offers instead a new theoretical basis for drama as a subject and a framework for dramatic practice. By acknowledging the importance of theatre culture as well as classroom culture to a balanced drama education, it proposes a dramatic curriculum based on the acceptance of drama's legitimate place within the arts and sets out to provide a structure for understanding education in drama in primary and secondary schools which will make sense to specialists and non-specialists as well as to students,[3] governors and parents.

A dramatic curriculum which pays careful attention to theatre practice will allow drama teachers access to a subject framework within which they will be able to focus on the quality of the dramatic product as well as on the issues disclosed by it. Other arts disciplines manage successfully to combine attention to form with concern about content, and there is no reason why this should mean a retreat into elocution classes and lectures on theatre history. As Peter Abbs comments, one of the problems with drama-in-education in the past was that a 'desire for immediate spontaneity of expression ousted stylistic constraints — and, hence, the formal possibilities — of inherited culture'.[4] In fact, experience suggests that sensitive induction into a culture of theatre with its conventions and accepted body of knowledge and skills is likely to stimulate rather than inhibit creative autonomy. Mastery of form goes along with the ability to express content, and form is only learned through experiencing a rich variety of options. Exposure to theatre culture should begin in the primary school.

Sadly, the relationship between classroom drama and the theatre world outside has never been as close as it should have been. Concentration in the early days upon the therapeutic benefits of drama for the participants diverted attention away from the idea of drama as communication to audiences. With the promotion of drama as a learning method in the 1970s the gap between school and theatre became more pronounced, and by the 1980s it had become customary in drama-in-education circles to speak of 'drama' and 'theatre' as two quite distinct categories of activity.[5]

Perhaps some of the popular myths about the theatre are partly to blame for past reluctance to embrace its conventions in school. Maybe grisly experiences of amateur performances dissuaded some teachers from incorporating theatre practice into their drama lessons. Certainly the school play has not always been the best advertisement for curriculum drama — inaudible voices, sagging scenery and hard chairs do not always inspire confidence in drama as an educational force. Meanwhile, the tendency of the popular press to publicize theatre gossip and highlight the seamier aspects of backstage life has not helped the image of theatre in schools.

Of course, the truth is that there are excellent amateur productions where all participants work hard and modestly to produce work of high quality by anyone's standards. By the same token, I know teachers who can coax extraordinary levels of achievement from young performers and technicians in school shows which, for intelligence, presentation and sheer artistic bravado, leave many professional productions standing. Also, while the professional theatre itself may have more than its fair share of misfits, the vast majority of actors are disciplined artists who use the talent they have been given and the skills they have acquired in the conscientious pursuit of their craft.

We must therefore be careful not to assume Rousseau's somewhat stereotypical view of the theatre as a place where 'in order to be temperate and prudent, we must begin by being intemperate and mad ...'[6] The days of the astrakhan coat and the cigarette holder, if they ever existed, are long gone. Many theatre workers are now employed by small companies which frequently share similar aims with teachers; some companies have active educational programmes. The links which might be made between schools — primary and secondary — and groups like these, as well as with companies which perform specifically for young people, are potentially very fruitful and will help to dispel the folklore.

If the dramatic curriculum is to reconcile drama in schools with its generic lineage by identifying fully with the theatre and its conventions, forms of practice and characterizing vocabulary, then changes will be inevitable. For one thing, the linguistic evasiveness of educational drama in matters theatrical will need to be displaced by a language more widely shared and understood. Like many disciplines fighting for recognition, drama-in-education has employed jargon to boost its esteem. Ever closer examination of the minutiae of the 'drama process' in journals and MA dissertations spawned a coded language to which few classroom teachers, I suspect, could honestly own access. The incorporation of this specialized language into an increasingly mystifying general discourse served to isolate drama-in-education not only from the rest of arts education, but also from the wider culture of the theatre. By contrast, in the new dramatic curriculum, student playwrights, directors, and stage-managers will tread the boards of the primary classroom as confidently as their professional counterparts do those of the local theatre; student actors will study their lines, rehearse their parts and perform, knowing that in doing so they join a tradition which stretches from ancient times to the dramas of their own experience.

It will have to be acknowledged that drama is a *performing* art. In the past, nervousness about the educational value of students performing has meant that drama-in-education's commitment to what might be assumed to be the most fundamental aspect of the subject — acting — has been sometimes less than whole-hearted. Nevertheless, from primary assemblies to examination practicals, students have continued to take on dramatic roles and act them out before audiences. For some students, their enthusiasm for drama will lead them to taking parts in the school play or in a youth theatre production. Drama teachers wary about the dramatic curriculum giving greater emphasis to this key element of dramatic art might seek reassurance from colleagues working in music or dance where the issue of performance has traditionally been less controversial.

Reservations about performing together with the domination of drama lessons by improvization and role-playing sometimes left only small spaces for the consideration of written texts, or playscripts. Although the 1980s saw the development of techniques for exploring scripts *through* drama, the emphasis here tended to be very much on the distillation of suitable themes and issues from published works. These then became the focus for more improvizations. That one might 'teach Shakespeare through drama' — an idea with much currency at the time — presupposed that classroom drama was best deployed in the unearthing of otherwise inaccessible aspects of the plays.[7] For all Peter Brook's conviction that 'the teaching is in the event not the message',[8] rarely was it suggested that it might also be appropriate to *perform* parts of a Shakespeare play in the classroom, despite the continuing popularity, in both primary and secondary schools, of 'extra-curricular' productions of Shakespeare.

This lack of attention to the written word meant that in many secondary schools with drama specialists, work on published plays happened mostly in the English department. This itself may well have reinforced in some students' minds the idea that playscripts were literature to be read around the class. However, in the same way that in music students from an early age learn to write and read musical scores, so the dramatic curriculum must accept playscripts as an essential part of the study of drama. Debate about themes and issues, about plays as literature, may well be the legitimate province of the English department; such discussion in drama, however, should be seen as a way of understanding and shaping possible interpretations of the plays in performance. Unlike English, drama can provide opportunities for the realization of those interpretations, with students actively directing, designing and performing. To reflect more accurately the key place of the playwright in the theatre tradition, the dramatic curriculum will have to redress the balance between scripted and devised work. As well as having opportunities to improvize as they progress in drama, students should be increasingly confronted by published work of all kinds.

Drama in schools has also been marked by a reluctance to engage with the process of skills acquisition. A tacit commitment to the tenets of progressive education persuaded many drama teachers in the 1980s to be wary of teaching 'theatre skills' in their lessons. Thus, as examination boards struggled to find assessment criteria which matched the broadly humanistic and developmental aims of drama-in-education, students being initiated into the rites of 'the drama process' were all too frequently left to their own devices when it came to making themselves heard and not falling over the scenery.[9] The result was that while those with some natural ability as performers would probably score quite highly, there was really no means of knowing how their less able peers were supposed to develop even quite basic drama skills. Other fundamental dramatic aptitudes were either only touched upon in passing or ignored altogether, and such commonplace features of theatrical life like set design, sound and lighting operation, administration, costume making and stage-management rarely made an appearance in drama lessons before A-level, let alone in the primary school. Yet skills like these are part of the very substance of drama at *all* levels. Taken together, they help to represent that body of knowledge, understanding and aptitudes which is dramatic art. Without their unabashed presence in schools, the dramatic curriculum will be seriously impoverished.

Other ghosts will also have to be exorcized. For example, for years drama-in-education at secondary level shrunk from the spectre of vocational training. To the student who might actually want to work in the theatre, the developmental vocabulary of 'the drama process' has little or nothing to say. Realistically, of course, few students achieve the status of professional actors. However, more might wish to pursue an interest awakened at school in an amateur capacity; for others, involvement in school drama may lead them into films or television, or into jobs as property makers, scene painters or theatre administrators. The extent of employment in arts-related industries in Britain is only just being acknowledged.[10] This is a vast area of potential interest for young people which drama-in-education has traditionally ignored.

Finally, a dramatic curriculum which seeks to locate itself within the arts community must address the question of drama's relationship with the other arts. Again, this is a matter about which drama-in-education has been largely silent. Yet the theatre is the one place where the arts regularly celebrate their commonality, with musicians, writers, dancers and designers collaborating on productions which consistently challenge the barriers which have grown up between the arts in Western culture. Dance-theatre, music-theatre and performance-art are all categories which break down the compartmentalization of the arts and by doing so enrich and diversify our experience. Students of dramatic art will need to know what an important place the other arts have in the making of dramas and the dramatic curriculum should demonstrate as eclectic and imaginative a range of artistic experience as the theatre itself.

Drama, English and the National Curriculum

Uncertainty about the nature of drama as an arts subject in the 1980s was matched by increasing confidence in the aims and methodologies of drama as a learning medium. The subsequent confusion which arose between the outcomes of learning *in* drama and learning *through* drama characterized the debate about drama in schools in the years leading up to the 1988 Education Reform Act. While large numbers of drama lessons were designed to examine a range of worthwhile issues and often incorporated highly sophisticated teaching and learning strategies, far fewer attempted to identify, much less monitor, how students actually got better at *drama itself.* The failure to resolve this key question of disciplinary identity only helped to secure drama's absence from the foundation subjects of the national curriculum.[11]

The promotion of dramatic learning methods involved drama making implicit claims on many areas of the school curriculum. Personal and social education, for example, was one field for which the processes of learning through drama seemed tailor-made. Students were able to play out a range of 'problem' situations in drama which offered up rich material for discussion. Some drama teachers came to believe that a principle aim of drama was to expose forms of social and historical oppression, such as racism and sexism, while generally there was a preoccupation with the exploration of topical issues of all kinds. Engagement in drama as an arts subject — sometimes disparagingly referred to as 'the mere study of theatre skills' — was subsumed within a wider educational agenda of social skills and political and moral awareness.

On the whole, drama syllabuses in secondary schools reflected this reluctance to engage with the substance of dramatic art. Instead, profiling schemes frequently highlighted matters of socialization and control by drawing attention to students' willingness to contribute to the lesson and work together in groups. Qualities like involvement and participation were given prominence and rated highly. Many of these non-subject-specific criteria were reflected in the new GCSE drama syllabuses which replaced the old CSE and O-level courses in 1986.[12]

While this emphasis on drama as a means to wider educational ends undoubtedly offered teachers across the curriculum a powerful new educational resource — one that has proved of particular value in the primary school — it distracted prominent practitioners and in-service education providers from the essential task of shoring up drama's eroding subject base. Over the years, in what seems to have been a systematic attempt to distance school drama from any identification with a subject-based theatre practice, 'theatre' words were discarded in favour of a self-contained methodological language. What most people know as 'acting' became 'acting out' or 'participating in an enactment' or 'role-playing', and while 'plays' were coyly referred to as 'drama fictions' in one GCSE syllabus, *the* 'role-play' became implicitly accepted as a noun in the lexicon of educational drama.

In fact, by the beginning of the 1980s 'role-playing' had become an all-embracing substitute for what happened when students temporarily surrendered their disbelief in order to enter the imagined world of the drama. Strictly speaking, being 'in role' is not quite the same as acting in the theatrical sense. Role, in drama-in-education, may be described as a way of using the imagination to try out what it might be like in someone else's shoes without having to complicate matters with attempts at rounded characterization. Thus, students together 'in role' may spontaneously improvize fictionalized versions of social, historical or moral dilemmas in ways which highlight the issues involved rather than the psychologies of those portrayed. Also, unlike stage acting, role-play is a readily accessible technique which requires no training or prior experience. Few adults will not at some time in their lives have consciously or unconsciously engaged in it.

The idea that role-play can be employed to help develop personal skills and explore social encounters of various kinds is now widely accepted. It is a technique commonly used in management training and in a plethora of courses designed to build confidence, relieve stress or encourage assertiveness. 'Role playing,' according to Professor Brian Cox, chair of the English Working Group, 'has become central to the courses and conferences that young executives go on'.[13] In secondary schools, role-play may be found in such diverse areas as special needs and multi-lingual education as well as personal and social education, and many primary teachers employ it as a matter of course in their day-to-day teaching.

It was undoubtedly drama's ownership of this valuable teaching tool that eventually gave 'the drama process' an important foothold in the national curriculum. Role-play was recommended as an aid to learning by many national curriculum foundation subject groups, but, most significantly, the English Working Group laid special emphasis on drama, recommending role-play 'specifically as a learning medium' in their speaking and listening programmes of study:

> . . . drama is one of the key ways in which children can gain an understanding of themselves and of others, can gain confidence in themselves as decision-makers and problem-solvers, can learn to function collaboratively, and can explore — within a supportive framework — not only a range of human feeling, but also a whole spectrum of social situations and/or moral dilemmas.[14]

In retrospect, for all the anguish and surprise expressed at the time, there is a remarkable consistency about the pattern of events which led to the endorsement of drama by the Cox Committee. A close historical relationship has meant that drama in schools has often seemed to have more in common with the aims of English than with the culture of theatre, and the fact that many well-known drama practitioners began their careers in

English departments is likely to have strengthened rather than challenged this affiliation.[15] The establishment of drama–in–education as a form of pedagogy (together with the fact that much drama in secondary schools is still taught within English departments) could only help to strengthen the bond between the two subjects. Acceptance by the Cox Committee of other drama techniques like 'hot seating', 'still pictures' and 'forum theatre' as valuable aids to the teaching of English meant that many of the drama methodologies developed during the 1980s became enshrined either in the government's statutory Order for English or the non–statutory guidance offered by the National Curriculum Council.[16]

Advocates of drama as learning, many of them true innovators, have some reason to be satisfied with the degree to which their efforts have been rewarded and we should not forget that for all the justifiable concerns about drama's lack of foundation subject status, some of the best principles of drama–in–education are now enshrined within the national curriculum. This is undoubtedly a tribute to all those who worked hard to ensure that drama should be firmly established in the educational consciousness.

It could be argued that faced by a government determined to re-introduce a version of the pre-war grammar school curriculum that this is the best that could have been hoped for. However, the fact must be faced that adherence to a particular set of methodologies in the 1980s set drama on a course which, while it looked at times as though it might elevate the subject to new educational heights, in fact lead it to a closer and closer identification with English. The task of this book is to rescue and secure those aspects of drama excluded from the national curriculum when the doors of English slammed shut.

Education in Drama

If drama in schools is to maintain an identity outside English, then the recognition of the arts as a discrete field within the curriculum — a field which need be no less coherent in concept and practice than that already successfully claimed by the sciences — is a necessary first step. It is only by drama teachers identifying closely with the push for whole arts policies in both primary and secondary schools that the future of drama as a recognized arts discipline may be reasonably assured.

This does not imply that the various arts should lose their separate identities — far from it. It is the principle informing the whole of the Falmer Press Aesthetic Library that the arts are not transferable; one or two art forms cannot stand in the place of all the others. Music is no substitute for dance nor visual art for drama; although linked generically, each form has its characterizing practices and modes of engagement. A balanced arts curriculum should allow students to have worthwhile experience of all art forms as well as offering opportunities for specialization. Drama teachers, accustomed to incorporating music, design and dance into their work, should be among the first to appreciate the educational benefits that practical cross-fertilization can bring.

Despite the 1980s' preoccupation with drama learning methodologies, there does seem to be a widely held view that drama has also every right to subject status. Also, of all the inconsistencies in the 1988 Education Reform Act, the apparently arbitrary distinction made in favour of art and music seems particularly thoughtless and unnecessary.[17] Indeed, as was pointed out at the time, the illogic of awarding only two art forms curricular legitimacy makes that decision a serious point of weakness in the rationale of the national curriculum itself. While to suggest that drama might be added to the list of foundation subjects would be to part company with the possible (if drama, then why not dance, or home economics, or media studies? — the waiting list for an already overcrowded curriculum is very long), to argue that every student has a right to a balanced arts education incorporating subjects from inside and outside the national curriculum is to base a workable idea on sound educational principle.

I believe that there is both justification and scope within existing frameworks for schools and local authorities to develop schemes which guarantee opportunities for students to have experience of all the arts during their years at school.[18] Of course, not all schools will see this as a priority; some may not consider it workable within present constraints, or even desirable. However, as arts advisers and inspectors well know, this is no radical departure. Headteachers with little or no interest in the arts will always find ways of pitching them out into porta-cabins and otherwise marginalizing them. The point is that the national curriculum does not in itself place a straitjacket on those who wish to sustain a balanced arts provision in their schools. At the same time, other requirements of the Education Reform Act, such as the devolution of school budgets and open enrolment, paradoxically may in some cases turn out to favour the arts. As schools become increasingly autonomous, previously indifferent headteachers may begin to realize how much the arts contribute to the ambiance of a school, that 'feel' of the place to which parents are so susceptible. I am convinced that the task of bringing the arts together to form a cohesive field within the curriculum can continue, even in an apparently inhospitable educational environment.[19]

Despite my reassurances, I appreciate that for some drama teachers the signposts towards a dramatic curriculum erected at the beginning of this chapter may seem unimaginative, even regressive, in their consistent reference to theatre practice. After all, they might still say, did not drama–in–education seek to forge itself an identity free from the shallow counterfeiting of painted scenery and Leichner No. 5? Were not the efforts of generations of committed practitioners directed towards the establishment of a form of education which eschewed the empty posturing of the theatre for the genuine, deeply felt, creative engagement of students with their own experience?

The trouble is, it appears that overwhelmingly students of all ages seem to enjoy being involved in the making and watching of plays. Nationally, drama schools continue to be flooded with applicants and participation in amateur and youth theatre has never been greater.[20] While audiences for professional theatre may not be what they were, the pervasiveness of modern technology means that millions now watch plays on television. Above all, as Martin Esslin points out, drama so infuses our understanding that it is now a key way of 'thinking about life'.

Drama has become one of the principal means of communication of ideas and, even more importantly, modes of human behaviour in our civilization: drama provides some of the principal role models by which individuals form their identity and ideals, sets patterns of communal behaviour, forms values and aspirations ...[21]

Embracing dramas of every kind — those that are played out on screens as well as those performed on stages — the programmes developed in this book will build on that peculiar human desire to take part in and to watch dramatic performances. While my proposals may well create some conceptual problems for those schooled in the language of dramatic pedagogy, they are nevertheless based upon practices which will not be unfamiliar to drama teachers. Too often in the past, impressive demonstration lessons have proved difficult, if not impossible, to translate to the ordinary primary classroom or secondary drama studio. Through the suggestions offered in this book, it is my hope that teachers will be able to regain some of their lost confidence with a curriculum that does not require the dazzling pedagogic skills of a super-teacher. Nothing of what follows should be beyond the scope of the ordinary teacher with a genuine interest in the theatre. At the same time, by identifying the making, performing and watching of plays as the fundamental elements of drama, and by encouraging classes to engage fully in all three, the dramatic curriculum places the creative responsibility firmly back in the hands of the students themselves.

The word 'culture' has already made an appearance or two in this chapter. As it will appear extensively in the pages that follow, readers should be clear that when I employ it I do not intend the word to suggest special categories of superior knowledge, or 'high art'. I rather use 'culture' to describe what Raymond Williams once called an 'assertion of a whole way of life'.[22] Culture, by this account, is a thickly woven tapestry of customs, forms of behaviour, beliefs and institutions which we inescapably inhabit as individuals and in which we find a collective identity; in Williams' words, 'culture is ordinary'.[23] We should remember, too, that in modern times, cultures are likely to be only partly bound by national boundaries; all of us belong to cultures which are simultaneously 'multi-cultures'. Also, as technology brings the furthest corners of the globe into our sitting-rooms, as well as our local cultural allegiances we cannot avoid regarding ourselves as part of a global culture. The importance of understanding the sense in which I employ the word 'culture' in my argument will become apparent in the following chapter.

The dramatic curriculum represents an attempt to restructure drama in schools so that drama's subject identity may be clearly articulated. Although what follows is specifically aimed at primary and secondary teachers, there is no reason why the structures proposed should not be extended into further education and beyond. They are intended to support a practical programme for education in drama which is clear, accessible and, above all, useful to drama teachers at all levels.

In the remaining chapters the shape of the dramatic curriculum will emerge. Because I believe that drama, like all the arts, has its roots in rational, social behaviour, I shall begin by proposing a theoretical basis for the study of dramatic art which attempts to reconcile the non-determinist, social outcomes of drama-in-education with an account of drama's origins in religion and its place in culture.

Notes and References

1 Department of Education and Science (1989b) *Drama from 5 to 16: HMI Curriculum Matters 17*, HMSO, p. 1.
2 For readers unfamiliar with the national curriculum, the 1988 Education Reform Act designated maths, English, and science as 'core' subjects, and history, geography, technology, physical education, music, art and a foreign language as 'foundation' subjects. Attainment in English covers 'reading', 'writing' and 'speaking and listening'. Learning-through-drama techniques figure prominently in the programmes of study for the latter, particularly in the National Curriculum Council's non-statutory guidance for English (1990a). See note 16 below.

3 Throughout this book I shall follow the Australian custom and refer to the recipients of education as 'students', whatever their age.

4 Abbs, P. (1987) *Living Powers: The Arts in Education*, London, Falmer Press, p. 44.

5 What became known as the 'drama or theatre' debate generated many column inches within the field. It was common to hear drama specialists talking of using 'theatre skills in drama' and attempts were made to draw up comparative tables. Underlying it all was an implicit assumption of the moral superiority of 'drama' over 'theatre'. For an examination of the origins of this peculiar dichotomy, see Hornbrook, D. (1989) *Education and Dramatic Art*, Oxford, Basil Blackwell.

6 See Rousseau, J-J. (1960) *Politics and the Arts: The Letter to M. d'Alembert on the Theatre* (translated by Allan Bloom), Glencoe, IL, Free Press, p. 20.

7 See Hornbrook, D. (1988) 'Shakespeare and educational drama', in Holderness, G., *The Shakespeare Myth*, Manchester, Manchester University Press.

8 'The simple reality is that *The Tempest* teaches directly through the quality of what is conjured up through the act of performance. The teaching is in the event not the message.' Brook, P. (1990) 'Theatre with a message? The very idea!' in *The Independent on Sunday*, 28 October.

9 At the height of enthusiasm for learning through drama, problems with knowing quite what to assess led to some strange inversions. In the absence of subject-based skills and knowledge, drama assessment schemes sometimes turned to the methodology of the 'drama process' itself. Thus, a technique like 'hot seating', for example, was transformed from a useful teaching technique to an assessment end. Students were graded according to their ability to participate in learning processes.

10 In 1990, over half a million people were employed in the arts industries in this country. For a breakdown of these figures and others relating to the economics of the arts, see Myerscough, J. (1988) *The Economic Importance of the Arts in Britain*, Policy Studies Institute, or its summary, Rodgers,

P. (1989) *The Work of Art: A Summary of the Economic Importance of the Arts in Britain*, London, Calouste Gulbenkian and Policy Studies Institute.

11 Despite fanciful claims that it was drama's formidable subversive potential that led to its deliberate suppression by the Tory government of the time, it seems certain that the national curriculum was simply copied from earlier models. Board of Education prescribed curricula for 1904 and 1935 resemble the 1988 national curriculum in almost every respect. See Aldrich, R. (1990) 'The National Curriculum: A historical perspective', in Lawton, D. and Chitty, C. (Eds) *The National Curriculum*, London, Institute of Education, pp. 22–3. However, the campaign to extend provision for music and art (singing and drawing in the 1935 version) to encompass all the arts was only narrowly lost. A stronger identification with this lobby by drama-in-education might have tipped the balance.

12 According to Andy Kempe's research into GCSE drama, 'awareness of and sensitivity to the group' is the only stated aim 'common to all of the major GCSE syllabuses' See Kempe, A. (1990) 'Odd Bed-Fellows', in *The Drama Magazine*, November, pp. 19–20.

13 Quoted in: Abrams, F. and Pyke, N. (1991) 'Arts face a cash squeeze', in *The Times Educational Supplement*, 18 January.

14 Department of Education and Science (1989a) *English for Ages 5 to 16* (The Cox Report), HMSO, para. 8.6.

15 These practitioners also tend to have English as opposed to drama degrees. In 1988, 26 per cent of those teaching drama had no qualification in the subject beyond A-level (*The Times Educational Supplement*, 13 October 1989).

16 Anyone who doubts the extent to which drama has been acknowledged within English should turn to the National Curriculum Council's non-statutory guidance on English. The chapter on drama incorporates, in summary, all the key elements of 'the drama process'. Improvization, 'teacher in role', 'person in role', forum theatre, investigative drama, ritual, 'mantle of the expert' and 'thought-tracking'

are all explicitly mentioned. See National Curriculum Council (1990a) *English: Non-Statutory Guidance*, D11–13.

17 See note 11 above.

18 The national curriculum handbook issued to all teachers by the Department of Education and Science, says: 'The foundation subjects are certainly *not* a complete curriculum; they are necessary but not sufficient to ensure a curriculum which meets the purposes and covers the elements identified by HMI and others.' Department of Education and Science (1989c) *National Curriculum: From Policy to Practice*, HMSO, para. 3.8.

19 The work of the Arts in Schools Project under the leadership of Ken Robinson, represents an invaluable contribution to this eminently sensible cause. Launched in 1985 by the School Curriculum Development Committee (SCDC), the Project completed its work in 1989 under the auspices of the National Curriculum Council. See National Curriculum Council (Arts in Schools Project) (1990c) *The Arts 5–16: Project Pack*, Harlow, Oliver and Boyd. See also, appendix 1.

20 In 1990, members of the Conference of Drama Schools received on average 1,500 applicants each for the twenty or so places at each school. In 1985, 15 to 16 million people in this country attended amateur dramatic performances (Policy Studies Institute, *op. cit.*).

21 Esslin, M. (1987) *The Field of Drama*, London, Methuen, pp. 13–14.

22 Williams, R. (1961) *Culture and Society, 1780–1950*, Harmondsworth, Penguin Books, p. 18.

23 See Williams, R. (1958) 'Culture is ordinary', reprinted in (1988) *Resources of Hope*, London, Verso.

Chapter 2

Understanding Drama

Wisehammer: How can I play Captain Brazen in chains?
Mary: This is the theatre. We will believe you.

Timberlake Wertenbaker, *Our Country's Good*, 1988[1]

Drama and the Arts

Historically, schools have included drama in the curriculum on
the basis of two implicit suppositions. One is that the subject is
part of the aesthetic field and therefore cannot reasonably
be excluded from a balanced arts education. The other is that
drama — at least in the forms commonly practised in schools —
is an independent developmental and pedagogic agent, embody-
ing in its special processes the fundamental premises of liberal,
or progressive, education.

Although neither of these ideas has ever been completely
absent from the discourse of school drama, ever since the earliest
pioneers the two claims have rivalled each other for precedence
among the theorists. Peter Slade advocated a dramatic version of
child art where displays of spontaneous theatricality seemed
incidentally to confirm the therapeutic effects of free expression.
Brian Way insisted that drama was primarily about making
better, more developed individuals and thought dramatic improvization would help towards the achievement of the general
good. In the 1980s, pedagogic versions of classroom drama saw

'art form' as very much the servant of a variety of social and moral issues.[2]

In practice, drama teachers have involved themselves in both what we might call the aesthetic and the developmental/pedagogic ends of school drama, although in the classroom the latter has tended to be pre-eminent. Thus, a teacher happy enough to immerse herself in after-school rehearsals for the annual musical might see no reason to bring the theatricality of this experience to the social or moral issues explored in her lessons. An emphasis on the pedagogic function of drama has meant that the introduction into the classroom of the theatrical skills and knowledge necessary for a performance has sometimes been represented as a betrayal of drama's role as an exploratory medium.

The roots of these distinctions are embedded in the historical circumstances by which drama came to be accepted as a legitimate part of education in Britain. Drama owes its very existence far less to a general acceptance of the arts as a generic within the curriculum than to the emergence of the idea of creative English in the 1950s and 1960s (as we have seen) and to historical changes like the raising of the school leaving age in 1972. Drama teachers have also a long history of devising strategies to accommodate the disaffected at the lower end of the ability range. This in turn has bred a strong identification with the premises of child-centred learning often supported by an explicit *political* commitment to the ideals of progressive education.[3]

The problem is that arts education in general has not been partial to aesthetic theories which concern themselves with the social or political context of art-making. Predominantly, arts educators have relied upon psychological accounts of creativity which place aesthetics beyond the reach of ideology. Such accounts suppose that there exists in all of us an inner faculty which governs our creative and aesthetic life and functions without any particular reference to the world outside. Indeed, supporters of this theory, like Robert Witkin, have argued that interference with the operation of this faculty, by critical engagement with students' work for example, is inherently damaging. Teachers who seek to influence the spontaneous creativity of students in any way can only inhibit the natural artist that lies within them. Under such a system, students paint or dance or improvize guided only by their own individual intuitive sense of 'rightness'.[4]

In this way, conflicting ideas about what art actually *is* have been largely circumvented. The idea of the artistic faculty directs attention away from the art object out in society and inwards towards the psychological process involved in its production; engagement by students in the 'art process' is judged to be intrinsically educative and life-enhancing. Indeed, the series of which this book is part is based upon the idea that there is something called the aesthetic field, 'an intricate web of energy', in which, one might say, all students have a right to graze.[5] While I find it difficult to disagree with this proposition and I shall return to it later, it nevertheless begs the question of how some experiences come to be in the field and others beyond its borders. How do I know that what I am experiencing is art?

The pervasiveness of this view of the aesthetic among educationalists may be one reason why some drama teachers have been wary of too close an identification with the arts; it is difficult to reconcile drama-in-education's commitment to the comprehensive educational objectives implied by the emphasis on pedagogy described in the previous chapter with the self-regarding relativism of a purely personal aesthetic of this kind.

Unfortunately, traditional, no-nonsense metaphysical accounts of artistic experience will be no more appealing to those who see drama as a vehicle for social change. Certainly, drama teachers are likely to be deeply sceptical of the hierarchical formalism of those academicians who try to reassure them about traditional values and mistrustful of the self-appointed custodians of 'high arts' who seem simply to know what art is.[6] An aesthetic theory based on the acceptance of established canons runs counter to both the intuitionism of Robert Witkin (anything goes so long as it is deeply felt) and the reformism of drama-in-education (drama is about social and moral issues).

When it comes to public discussions about art, most western Europeans probably subscribe to a rough and ready consensus in which certain individuals — David Hockney, Jane Austen, Mozart, to pick some at random — are recognized as artists and what they produce as art. However, people will be far less sure of their categories when confronted by less familiar projects. The incomprehension of the general public faced with a piece of apparently shapeless sculpture or with a decision to fund someone to carry a pole on his head across Norfolk is widely shared. Art-works of this kind are often unsettling because they challenge the 'common-sense' view of what is, and is not, art.

One way of dealing with this is simply to assert that our experience of art is purely subjective; all art is simply an expression of a private preference. This kind of existential bravado is very common. 'Well, for me, it's not art', dismisses a work irrefutably. Unfortunately, as a theory of art it will not altogether do; a version of what I have called elsewhere the 'True for Me' argument, it rests upon a mistake about the use of words.[7] The speaker is confusing a judgment about quality with the acceptance of language categories. For the word 'art' to justify its place in our shared vocabulary, its utterance must conjure those tacitly agreed kinds of human enterprise we have come to call 'the arts'. Thus, although I might legitimately say that (for me) the man with the pole in Norfolk is not art (meaning, that in my view, there is not yet sufficient agreement over the inclusion of work of that kind in the arts category) I cannot on similar grounds claim that the works of Turner are not art (in the face of overwhelming agreement that they are). Of course, although Turner's paintings are irrefutably art, whether I *like* them or not is another matter. The conclusion to be drawn from this is that questions about what is and is not art cannot therefore be left to each individual's subjective response.

If art is not simply a matter of subjective preference but rather a question of agreement over language, is it possible to identify and formalize the criteria for such agreement? We could then surely measure each new artistic experience against these criteria and make our decision. By agreement (our argument might then go) a Brahms symphony is art so music that resembles it must also be art; Constable's landscapes hang in the most respectable galleries so paintings that look like Constable's must be art too. While plausible to an extent, the danger of this 'common-sense' approach to art is that it can too easily become stultifying, culturally confined and traditionalist in the worst possible sense. For example, most of the painting produced in Germany between 1933 and 1945 was 'common-sense' in this way, what we would recognize now as little more than sentimental pastiche. Artists whose work disturbed those assiduously attempting to mould popular sentiment at the time — Brecht, Weill and Piscator among them — fled abroad; those who remained subordinated themselves to the political climate and became derivative, predictable and safe. Popular assumptions about art are nevertheless heavily influenced by this 'common-sense' perception. That is perhaps one reason why in Western societies there is generally a gulf between Williams' 'ordinary culture' and some of the art that appears in concert-halls, galleries and theatres. Objects and events which common sense tells us are art and which are accorded suitable status by society may actually have no genuine cultural resonance at all.

Perhaps all we can be certain of is that the shifting and often imprecise nature of the language in which we express our views and organize our categories will ensure that what is and what is not art will remain in dispute. Apart from anything else, in the English language the word 'art' carries a vast range of meanings. 'Artful' and 'artistic' are not at all the same thing and 'art' itself is equally capable of signifying skill at football as it is a work of aesthetic importance. If we get as far as conceding that we limit ourselves to 'works of art', then the problem is hardly made easier. In Karen Blixen's story, *Babette's Feast*, for example, the author celebrates the work of her heroine, once chef at the Café Anglais, as a work of art; reading of the feast's sumptuousness, the consummate skill of its preparation and the simple humility with which it is served, it is difficult to disagree. In the public domain, 'art' has an elasticity which makes it hard to confine.[8]

While it is clearly beyond the scope of this book to attempt to resolve the dilemmas I have raised here, problems about what we might mean by art when we talk about education in the arts have at least to be acknowledged before we embark upon a programme for education in drama. As it is, I think it is probably fair to say that arts education has implicitly embraced a more or less 'common-sense' view. By rendering opaque the debate about the social formation of art, art-as-educational-process hides its dependence upon cultural agreement and attempts to disguise the assimilation of art into the material and ideological structures of society. In this way, the formative role of culture and history is tacitly accepted but the material basis of art then becomes invisible under claims of universality which are really tacit assumptions about consensus. While an illusory transcendence may sometimes suit the purposes of classroom drama it has small purchase on the reality of life in the arts outside the school. Here, amid their battles for recognition and resources, actual practising artists — actors included — will too often find themselves struggling for survival in a world which is nothing if not starkly material.

Without pretending that we can come up with definitive solutions to the categorical dilemmas raised by this briefest discussion of the nature of art, I do think it is possible to arrive at a serviceable account of the kinds of things we call art — in particular of those categories of art we call drama — which will satisfy a requirement to acknowledge the social and political dimension of the arts as well as the aesthetic. For such an account to be useful to drama teachers it should not set out so much to *define* drama — to draw a defensive line around it — but rather to *describe* and explain the kinds of thing drama is. A story of drama-as-art of this kind may help to reassure those teachers who remain committed to the radical moral and social aims of drama education and at the same time lead (hopefully) to greater complexity and concern with philosophical and ideological matters among those for whom dramatic art is unproblematically that which happens in theatres.

If we believe that drama should stir the thoughts and feelings of students — and has the potential to do so very deeply — then an account of drama-as-art of this kind must find some way of combining the resonances of everyday life which are their common experience — their 'ordinary culture' — with the genuinely 'extra-ordinary' experience that seems to accompany engagement with art. There is no reason why drama should not have its roots in the everyday while still retaining the capacity to affect profoundly the way we think, feel and act.

Acting and Believing

The history of any word is the history of its use. That 'art' means this for one society and that for another, that for each its meaning will have changed over time, that in some cultures no equivalent word for 'art', let alone 'drama', exists, all suggest that any easy consensus over this subject will elude us.

The only commonality which is immediately apparent is the connection in all cultures at some time in their history, between art and religion. The basis of my argument here is that the key which unlocks the secret of the mysterious power drama and the other arts have for us is to be found at that point in the development of human societies when religious belief is displaced by competing accounts of reality.

I make no apologies, therefore, for examining the significance of early cultures for the emergence of those characteristic activities which we call drama. However, in doing so my purpose is not to plod remorselessly along that well-trodden progress from the rain dance to the Royal Opera House. I wish rather to assemble for teachers an account of drama which is intelligible as aesthetic theory (I shall thus continue to speak of dramatic art) but which at the same time satisfies the social and moral tradition exemplified by the so-called 'issue-based' drama of the 1980s.

In the years following the Second World War, dissatisfaction with the dominant forms of European theatre led to a developing interest among European theatre practitioners in the rituals of ancient communities. In a search for an alternative drama, writers like Antonin Artaud and experimental directors like Peter Brook and Jerzy Grotowski, turned to ancient forms in an attempt to discover and recreate a more fundamental expression of our innate dramatic powers. From the trance-inducing liturgies of the dance, the masked worshippers and fantastically costumed shamans possessed of the spirit of the gods, they hoped to distil something of the very essence of humanity, something so basic, so incontrovertibly *natural*, that it would awaken a spirit numbed by years of exposure to what Brook called 'deadly theatre'.

By the end of the 1960s, substantial numbers of freshly trained drama teachers emerging from their colleges were making similar connections. Proselytes of the bright, new discipline, Drama-in-Education, these young men and women opposed not only the literary domination of English theatre, but also, in many cases, the whole conventional structure of performer/audience relationship. The trust games and dance-dramas of the 1960s drama class often reflected the same search for authenticity abroad in alternative theatre, a search that could be recognized in Artaud's sacrificial manifestos or witnessed in the heady mix of Zen, marijuana and psychoanalysis of Julian Beck's *Living Theatre*.

The sober 1980s saw the music and coloured light which once transformed a bleak school hall into a magical arena displaced by less festive, if more focused, approaches to drama. Role-play in all its forms swept away the props, costumes and other paraphernalia, the dramatic presence of the teacher being deemed sufficient to supply the necessary mood and tension for the ceremony. Outside, where fringe and mainstream had become virtually indistinguishable, the mood had changed too. Innovatory writers and directors turned elsewhere for inspiration. Brook's magnificent *Mahabharata* stood out as a lonely reminder of his continuing quest for an essential dramatic language.

Despite this general retreat, it is widely accepted that the origins of drama, and indeed all art, lie in the religious rites of our distant ancestors. That there might be a connection between drama and ritual is not difficult to see. The post-war interest in the ritualized forms of African and Asian liturgical story-telling was inspired not so much by anthropological inquisitiveness but rather by a belief that, in an important sense, dramatic and religious experiences were of a similar order. Brook advanced the idea of 'holy theatre', Grotowski advocated the 'holy actor'. Few who have been deeply affected by a drama would deny that the experience is almost impossible to describe, that sometimes it does really seem, in some important sense, spiritual.

What is it, then, that resonates so powerfully within us when we engage successfully with art that it sometimes *feels* like a religious experience? What leads us to use words like 'spiritual' to describe drama that moves us greatly? Is it possible to reconcile the profundity of these experiences with an otherwise rationalist outlook?

Examining the activities of the shaman, or witch-doctor, of the Cuna tribe in Panama, the anthropologist Claude Lévi-Strauss notes that the shaman has a method of easing a difficult child-birth by reciting and performing a long incantation. According to Cuna mythology, a difficult child-birth results when Muu, the power responsible for the formation of the fetus, exceeds her functions and captures the *purba* or soul of the mother-to-be. The song tells the story of the quest for the lost *purba*, a quest which culminates in the defeat of Muu and her daughters by the shaman and his tutelary spirits, and the restoration of the *purba* to the ailing woman.[9]

The efficacy of this pain-relieving exercise depends upon the sick woman believing in the myth of Muu and upon her belonging to a society which believes in it. The shaman, and the belief system he serves, are providing the woman with a language through which she can express the previously inexpressible.

> The tutelary spirits and malevolent spirits, the supernatural monsters and magical animals, are all part of a coherent system on which the native conception of the universe is founded. The sick woman accepts these mythical beings or, more accurately, she has never questioned their existence.[10]

Although psychological, in the sense that it involves the exorcism of one person's pain, the cure is also heavily and essentially, *social*. Its effectiveness depends not on the power of one person's subjective faith but on the collective faith of the society of which she is part. It is this *inter*-subjective belief that is harnessed to do the job. If the sufferer does not subscribe to the mythology then the shaman is powerless. If she does, then the power of the group, through the shaman, is startling. In these circumstances, it could be argued that belief like this is perfectly rational.

The means by which the shaman exercises his power is ritualized narrative. He offers a version of the myth which sustains the belief system of the group. To a casual observer (were such a thing possible), his performance may resemble that of a frenetic actor. However, to interpret these events as a form of drama is to misunderstand what is going on between the shaman and the other members of the tribe.

To this day, Roman Catholics believe that in the Eucharist the bread and wine are transubstantiated into the body and blood of Christ, only their appearance remaining. That is to say, the bread and wine do not perform a symbolic function; they really do become flesh and blood. The same kind of belief pertains in relation to the true shaman. He does not *represent* the myth in his incantation; he actually *lives* it, becomes the god. He does not, as an actor would, 'put himself in the place' of the spirits he expresses. The true shaman believes in his transubstantiation, and this belief is shared by the community he serves.

Similarly, the response of the shaman's witnesses is fundamentally different from that of a theatre audience. Within a theatre, messages flow from performers to individuals, who may or may not pick them up, who may or may not become in some way emotionally involved in the play and who may or may not act differently as a result of their experience. Rituals, such as the pain-easing one cited above, on the other hand, are directed for very specific purposes. Ceremonies evolve to ensure victory in wars, or to appease the elements or to encourage good harvests. The ritual not only embodies the hopes and aspirations of an entire community but is expressed in a language through which that community makes sense of its experience of the world. Again, within the context of such a community, and so long as the rituals continue to be effective, to participate in these belief systems is not necessarily irrational.

At the same time, belief like this is rarely a matter of choice. Generally speaking, we simply grow up amongst the rituals which sustain us and give our lives meaning. For all of us, the language through which understanding is articulated governs the limits of understanding itself. As Wittgenstein says, we are bound by the vocabularies which constitute the statements we make about reality. These vocabularies are not restricted to spoken language, but cover that network of signs used by members of a society to communicate and over whose meaning there must be tacit agreement. Here, in the ritual of the shaman, we are confronted by a complex system of signifiers made up of words, movements and mythological narratives. From the perspective of the tribe, to question them on anything but their own terms is to behave incomprehensibly. Like us, the Cuna are bound by the limits of their vocabulary.

For a variety of reasons, few self-contained communities like the Cuna remain. The vast majority of us belong to societies which have long lost their cultural and religious homogeneity. The fragmentation of communities of belief and the subsequent infiltration of once rational belief structures by secular interests can lead to ideological and epistemological tensions over which there can sometimes seem no possibility of common ground. I remember once using some simple role-play to help explain this to students. Asking them to imagine they were Galileo rushing from his telescope with the evidence that the earth was not, after all, the centre of the universe, I would take the part of a sympathetic but devout monk. Their task was to persuade me of the truth of the discovery. For the students, with their post-Enlightenment consciousness, the evidence of their eyes was sufficient; as the monk, I wanted to know if, by refuting the teaching of the Church in this way, they were doubting the scripture, possibly the very existence of God. Where in the holy scripture, I would ask them, does it say that the earth is simply one of many planets circling the sun? Despite (to our thinking) the apparent incontrovertibility of Galileo's position, the result was, of course, always an impasse. To Galileo, the monk was simply blind to what was self-evident; to the monk, Galileo was a heretic.

I do history a deep injustice, of course, with this simplification. By the early seventeenth century dogma and empiricism had a far more complex relationship than indicated by this little exercise and my devout monk could hardly be said to represent the Church establishment of the time — resistance to change had more to do with secular power than religious observance. Nevertheless, the confrontation does perhaps serve to illustrate my point. We are all anchored within belief systems, and for a self-sufficient, stable society, these systems are articulated by the shamans or priests and embodied in the shared rituals. What happens when these communities of belief begin to break down is the key to understanding our relationship with art.

Drama as a Cultural System — The Grounded Aesthetic

From a rationalist viewpoint, religions are collections of practices and beliefs originally devised by communities to help them survive in a hostile and unpredictable world. Their followers exhibit what Wittgenstein calls 'a passionate commitment to a system of reference'.[11] Religion may be regarded as simply a way of extending rationality from the ordinary tasks of our daily lives which rely on the predictability of the physical world to those other areas of our experience where what we sometimes call 'fate' seems to play such an important part; pain, bereavement, disease, unexpected good luck, the prospect of our own death. In its simplest form, religion tells us stories which give accounts of the unpredictable and help to draw the unknown into the known. Thus, the rituals of the Cuna represent a particular means of understanding and attempting to control an apparently random universe.

Put another way, we can say that all religions start off as forms of *usefulness*. A story of life after death, for example, is useful in this sense because it explains the puzzle of our ultimate non-existence; a story of life after death which incorporates a system of punishment and reward (hell and heaven) is doubly useful, for it also prescribes the rules by which we must live. Success in telling useful stories of this kind is one reason why religion has survived into the modern age.

As cultures develop, traditional stories tend to be superseded by others which have proved themselves to offer more useful explanations. In this process, because most of our actions are based upon a rough-and-ready logical empiricism, logical empiricism tends to triumph over metaphysics as cultures advance. Once we know the story of static electricity the idea of a supernatural being throwing thunderbolts becomes a redundant account of reality; it ceases to be of use to us in explaining the world. A tension then arises because the language through which a culture tells stories about itself cannot adapt as rapidly as the stories themselves. Thus, while an electrostatic theory of lightning may, for practical purposes, explain things more satisfactorily to a culture which up to that point had believed in thunderbolts, the explanation itself will still only make sense if expressed in the language of thunderbolts. While the culture may now *believe* in electricity, its *sensibility*, as expressed in the language of the stories it tells, still incorporates the existence of the supernatural being.

An incongruence subsequently develops between the practical business of moving about the world and the stories that are told about it. Of course, over time the language used to describe experience will itself adapt and change and new stories will emerge as fresh agreements over meaning are tacitly reached. However, as with my Galileo example, there will always be a tension between our experience as we are experiencing it and our ability to articulate it, between what we consciously believe (what we say we 'know' to be the case) and the collective sensibility to which we unconsciously, but necessarily, subscribe. In a stable society, this tension will be small or nonexistent; for the Cuna, the degree of correspondence between myth and reality may be virtually absolute. In societies exposed to rapid change, on the other hand, the tension may be very great indeed (in Galileo's case, requiring public refutation under threat of torture). As cultural systems begin to fragment, under the influence, possibly, of rival stories offering more useful explanations, then the tension between the residual forms of belief which shape cultural sensibility and the emergent forms often surface in what we would now recognize as art.

European history in particular provides us with abundant examples of this process. Indeed, I would argue that it is the presence of tensions of this kind which bequeaths European society stories of paradox and ambiguity, dramas of uncertainty and irresolution, stories notably absent from the healing myths of the Cuna. Shakespeare, for example, a playwright himself caught at the disjuncture between the old stories of the Middle Ages and the emergent ones of the Renaissance, shows us a

Danish prince paralyzed by his inability to choose between them. We have too, in the drama of Classical Greece, a vivid example of the emergent dialectic between sensibility and belief characteristic of a society in which an advancing secularism is played out on a religious stage. The legendary Thespis, who detached himself from the dithyramb chorus in late sixth century Athens, and who in doing so was the first unsanctified person to assume the character of a god, stands at the point of transition in Greek culture from mystic ritual to drama, from religion to art. With Thespis, the shaman breaks his magic staff and becomes an actor. Later, as Athenians watched the climax of Aeschylus' *Orestia*, they witnessed the symbolic judgment of Orestes being performed by an Athenian jury, the casting vote being that of the goddess Athena herself. In *The Eumenides*, the avenging Furies are not defeated by other spirits, as in the shaman's battle with Muu, but agree to be integrated into the young Athenian democracy: 'Force is needless; let persuasion check/The fruit of foolish threats ...'[12] Still held within the context of a religious festival in honour of gods whose exploits form the narrative, the experience in the Periclean Theatre was a celebration, in versions of the old mythological stories, of the new, more useful, but secular story of Athenian nationalism and civic self-regard.

But what of non-European traditions? Do they exhibit similar tensions? Anthropologist Clifford Geertz warns that when talking about art our implicit, 'common-sense' commitment to a European perspective of enlightenment aesthetics (and what he calls, that rather peculiar notion of 'fine arts') has blinded us, rather like my imaginary monk, to the multiplicity of ways art is regarded in non-Western societies. Thus, when we are confronted by work that displays all the characteristics of art as we know it we are puzzled if, within the culture which produced the work, there seems to be no concomitant language to talk about it. A closer examination of this apparent paradox may throw some light on the subtle interrelationship between religion, art and culture.

Geertz tells the story of the Tiv, 'aimlessly sewing raffia onto cloth', who explains: 'If the design does not turn out well, I will sell it to the Ibo; if it does, I will keep it; if it comes out

extraordinarily well, I shall give it to my mother-in-law'.[13]
What are we to make of this? Is it really sensible for us with our
Enlightenment consciousness to re-describe the work in terms
of, shall we say, its 'feeling form' or its contribution to some
contrived primitive canon? And yet, the Tiv, by all his actions
(including the apparent purposelessness of the activity and its
outcome) certainly *seems* to be making art. He has a clear understanding that, when completed, the work will be judged favour-
ably or unfavourably and he clearly subscribes, if only tacitly, to
the scale of values by which judgment will be made.

Similarly, in his study of the Balinese cockfight, Geertz
ponders over the possible significance of this 'drama' to those
who participate in it. The connection between cockfighting and
demonistic powers is explicit in the ritual blood sacrifice of this
traditional contest, but as Geertz discovered, the fights are also
immensely complex forms of social expression. The cocks
themselves are subject to elaborate ceremonial preparation and
the wagering on the fights is conducted according to strict rules
of status. To Western eyes, the spectacle of steel-spurred cocks
tearing each other to pieces for wagers may be profoundly
disquieting. Yet the persistence of the cockfight, despite its
illegality, Geertz sees as evidence of its powerful hold on the
imagination of the Balinese.

Geertz concludes that for the Tiv and the Balinese the
activities described are symbolic actions which, despite their
apparent arbitrariness (in the case of the Tiv) and violence (in the
case of the cockfight), give meaning to the participants.

> ... the cockfight renders ordinary, everyday experience
> comprehensible by presenting it in terms of acts and
> objects which have had their practical consequences
> removed and been reduced (or, if you prefer, raised)
> to the level of sheer appearances, where their meaning
> can be more powerfully articulated and more exactly
> perceived ... What it does is what, for other peoples
> with other temperaments and other conventions, *Lear*
> and *Crime and Punishment* do ...[14]

For Geertz, the cockfight is a 'metasocial commentary', a dramatized story the Balinese tell about themselves. The cockfight interprets the culture in confirmatory metaphors of blood, crowds, status and death, metaphors which shape, and which in turn are shaped by, the language of the culture itself. To the Balinese the spectacle is not just entertainment or the opportunity for a flutter, but a form of deep cultural confirmation.

Both these examples give us a further purchase on the idea that 'art' may usefully be said to describe what are essentially culturally bound objects and practices whose meaning is located, like that of religion, in the gap between our experience as members of a culture and our ability as individuals to articulate it. By this account, the cockfight is no less art than those dramas which give meaning to our own social identities in similar ways, but which we are accustomed to seeing in theatres (or classrooms). I would argue that engagement in drama or any art is not possible unless we are part of that 'general system of symbolic forms', that collective sensibility, which constitutes the culture which produced it. Our capacity to perceive meanings in dramas — cockfights, classical tragedies, classroom improvizations — can only be a product of our collective experience. In the secular society, art replaces religion as the predominant form of symbolic usefulness.

To describe these living symbolic forms as they occur in modern societies, Paul Willis has proposed the term *grounded aesthetic*.

> [Grounded aesthetic] is the creative element in a process whereby meanings are attributed to symbols and practices and where symbols and practices are selected, re-selected, highlighted and recomposed to resonate further appropriated and particularized meanings.[15]

Willis argues that whereas the received sense of the aesthetic (as in 'high arts') sentimentalizes art by emphasizing 'the cerebral, abstract or sublimated', the grounded aesthetic is concerned with the production of meanings and explanations 'in relation to concrete conditions and situations'. Like Geertz,

Willis believes that these meanings provide us with 'collective and personal principles of action' while at the same time holding and repairing the 'precariousness and fragmentedness' of identity itself.[16] From cockfights to community plays, those symbols and practices which constitute the grounded aesthetic are forms of usefulness similar to the belief structures of the Cuna. The grounded aesthetic draws meaning from our collective sensibility and is rooted as irrevocably in the life of the cultures to which we belong as it is in the language with which we communicate.

It has been pointed out, notably by Marxist critics, that the powerful influence exerted by the sensibility of a society on the beliefs and actions of its members, invites attempts at secular control. Indeed, as sensibility declares itself in ideology through those recognizable structures of ideas embodied in a society's institutions, symbolic forms are open to manipulation by those whose interests are served by the sustaining of old beliefs. The false shaman who knows his business will exert great power over the tribe to his own advantage; the corrupt Church, as Luther knew, will not easily relinquish its control over entry into the heavenly kingdom, even if it involves the sale of indulgences; capitalism, or at least, those who profit by it, will not shrink from exploiting cultural forms in its drive for greater consumption.

In response to this some theorists have claimed that art is legitimate only as the manifestation of deep truths. Art which tells lies about the world, such as fascist painting, they would argue, is in reality only pseudo-art. While there is some force to this argument — the sense of heightened reality we often experience in the presence of art can sometimes seem powerfully revelatory (I shall have more to say about this in a moment) — according to my thesis so far, art is no more true nor false than religion. The kind of truth art is, like the kind of truth religion is, can only be manifest in the shared language of a culture, in its visual as well as its linguistic metaphors, in its dramatic semiology and in its music. By this token, there are no super-cultural objective standards against which the truth or falsity of art may be judged. The extent to which art is truth is only the extent to which it engages with the sensibility of the culture, the extent to which it seems to be saying important things to us, things which are useful to us as we attempt to understand the world and our place within it.

In modern societies, a nation's culture — that collection of customs, beliefs and forms of behaviour which cumulatively give a society its collective identity — is likely to be the product of widely disparate elements each with its own cultural identity. We may speak of Great Britain, therefore, as being a culture which is at the same time truly 'multi-cultural', its various elements preserving something of their ethnographic separateness while contributing to and receiving from the whole. We are now also increasingly members of a world culture. Rapid communication and dissemination mean that we no longer marvel at the idea of a Japanese concert pianist and that to witness, shall we say, a Balinese cockfight, we may need only to reach for the remote control. This paradox of unity and disunity, of a developing global culture and fragmenting local ones, where, in Marx's words, 'all that is solid melts into air', is a characterizing feature of modern life and of the art which attempts to make sense of it.

> Modern environments and experiences cut across all boundaries of geography and ethnicity, of class and nationality, of religion and ideology: in this sense, modernity can be said to unite all mankind. But it is a paradoxical unity, a unity of disunity: it pours us all into a maelstrom of perpetual disintegration and renewal, of struggle and contradiction, of ambiguity and anguish.[17]

We must face the fact that art cannot escape the maelstrom of modernity. While this may make art no less the potential vehicle of deception than any other cultural form, it also ensures that cultural sensibility will never surrender completely to the blunt instrument of political control. Nowadays, technology has given most of us access to meaning-bearing symbolic forms which are simply too diffuse to be comprehensively manipulated in this direction or that, however skilful the ideological engineers.

However contradictory and confusing they may be, the

grounded aesthetic locates art firmly amongst the confirmatory metaphors of everyday life and in doing so offers us an account which links culture and experience and brings art squarely into the social realm. By doing so, I believe it provides education in drama with a theoretical foundation for classroom practice which will help to reconcile the social, moral and political aims of drama-in-education with the aesthetic programmes of dramatic art represented by the dramatic curriculum.

Aesthetic Recognition

In schools, the idea of dramatic art as a cultural system deeply embedded in the way we think and feel and make sense of the world will mean a shift of emphasis away from the quasi-therapeutic school drama of the past where social and developmental ends often prevailed, and towards a dramatic curriculum based upon the experience of culture and rooted in our collective sensibility. Within such a curriculum, drama teachers share their knowledge and skills with the students, opening up for them a lexicon of dramatic art which stretches across the world and from the earliest human communities. However idiosyncratic or 'non-relevant' a teacher's enthusiasm for drama may be, a genuine excitement about drama stands a chance of stimulating the experience which I believe lies at the heart of arts education — *aesthetic recognition.*

It is generally acknowledged that students do not learn in the arts in the same way that they learn in other curriculum areas. Because of the unpredictable nature of the arts, there are important aspects of aesthetic education which clearly cannot be approached with familiar incremental models of learning. Students do not necessarily become more creative as they grow older. Furthermore, there are many adults who would now count themselves as possessors of a deep and lasting interest in the arts who had no significant arts education at school at all and come from homes distinctly lacking in what Pierre Bourdieu calls 'cultural capital'.[18]

So how is it that we come to make those connections with culture which we call artistic experience and which can direct us to a long and edifying association with a particular art form? For arts educators, this is surely a most fundamental question. After some informal research among adults, David Hargreaves noticed that many people seem to acquire what we might call 'a love of art' as the result of a strikingly vivid inductive experience. For no reason that he could discern, contact with a work of art about which they apparently had no prior knowledge had affected some of his sample so profoundly that they could only describe the experience as 'religious'. Hargreaves called this sudden initiation into an art form, a 'traumatic conversion'.[19]

The idea of an initial conversive experience is certainly consistent with the relationship between art and religion I have already proposed. However, while acknowledging the evidence of Hargreaves' research I would interpret his findings slightly differently. We can explain this phenomenon without recourse to psychology or religion by placing experiences of this kind within the context of the grounded aesthetic.

What occurs during the 'traumatic conversion' is in fact only an extreme version of what happens to all of us when, as it were, we are taken off our guard by art; we are startled by a profound sense of recognition. As members of a culture, we will unconsciously internalize the sensibility of that culture in ways determined by our individual biographies. Hargreaves' conversive trauma can thus be re-interpreted as the experience of an instant in time when elements of this internalized sensibility suddenly coincide with their representations in the culture itself and burst vividly into our consciousness — when, in Wittgenstein's words, we 'resonate in harmony' with a work of art.[20] It is true that this sense of harmony is also a feature of religious conversion and may seem by the subject to be revelatory in the same way. However, as I have argued that both religion and art are forms of usefulness with strong residual components, this similarity is not surprising. Deep religious experiences, like artistic ones, confirm a powerful, identity-sustaining sense of membership.

Thus, while Hargreaves' aesthetically deprived adults may not have had BBC Radio Three playing in the house when they were children, they were nevertheless inescapably members of a society in which school hymns, military marches, rock music and television commercials resonated with the particular tropes and harmonies of the European musical tradition. It is doubtful that an Indonesian family familiar only with the characteristic tuning systems of Balinese music would experience a sudden conversion to Wagner in the way Hargreaves describes. However, it is not so difficult to see how a child who has unconsciously absorbed a dense vocabulary of musical understanding might one day be touched deeply by a piece which for some reason connects what has been internalized to contemporary experience.

For drama teachers, the lesson to be learned from this is that the motivation for resonant engagement in dramatic art is likely to be provoked by an experience of aesthetic recognition in work *external* to the students themselves. Deep learning in drama may well be more profoundly accomplished by asking students to watch a play than by encouraging them to participate in one. For this reason, the dramatic curriculum will need to be served by a rich and varied programme of external stimuli. It certainly cannot be assumed that aesthetic recognition will occur when the diet is most obviously 'relevant'. The limited agenda of 'issues' characteristic of a certain kind of drama lesson often plays to a narrow parochialism which confines rather than releases students' imaginations. Experience suggests that the moment of recognition when representation and sensibility collide is at least as likely to be induced by a Verdi opera as by *Kes*, by the *Mahabharata* as by a visiting show about youth culture.

An account of art as a cultural system requires a dramatic curriculum in schools which is both flexible and eclectic. This will mean opening up the drama lesson to as wide a range of dramatic experience as possible and allowing students to experiment within a context which acknowledges the broader culture (and cultures) of which they are of necesssity members. By doing so, drama teachers may be assured that the political and social aims of drama will not be neglected, for our 'common culture' incorporates dissent as much as it does acquiescence.[21] By locating drama in this fertile landscape not only is aesthetic recognition more likely but the possibilities for expanding students' knowledge and understanding are vastly enhanced. The dramatic curriculum should embrace not only that which happens in theatres or drama classrooms, but all the varied manifestations of dramatic form to which we are exposed. In this way, school drama's wide pedagogic agenda will be assured of a secure place within a broadly defined aesthetic framework.

Summary — Drama as Art

By drawing a distinction between religion and art, between ritual and drama, while at the same time acknowledging art's liturgical antecedents, I have tried to show that the sensibility of our secular society has its distant origins in what were once rational and above all *useful* beliefs, and that the residue of these beliefs continues to inform the way we think, feel and express our ideas.

We know that humans, unlike other animals, engage in the kinds of activity we like to call art. The human species developed gregariously, forming tribes or communities the members of which were of necessity interdependent. In order to survive, our distant ancestors had to make sense of the world as it presented itself to them in ways which worked. Their explanations had, above all, to be practical. To preserve the cohesiveness of the group, these explanations were probably initially the result of agreement. Later, they would be incorporated into the inherited language of the group and passed onto successive generations as stories, a form of collective autobiography. Ritualized versions of these stories enacted by shamans made sense of the overwhelmingly contingent nature of primitive life and provided a matrix of belief which eventually became buried in the discourse of the tribe.

Such evidence we have of the forms of these rituals is easily mistaken for art. The Paleolithic cave drawings in the cavern of the Trois-Frères, for example, might be taken for rather inept depictions of a hunt. However, closer examination reveals something of their magic purpose and allows us to speculate as to the use to which they may have been put. Similarly, while the shamanic pain relieving dance may have the characteristics of a dramatic performance it is probably more appropriate to interpret it as a form of alternative medicine.

Eventually, these 'making sense' rituals became systematized as religions, with gods, substantiating narratives and officiating priests. In these communities of agreement — that is, agreement to believe in the practical efficacy of certain procedures, explanations and so on — there would be a close correspondence between the beliefs a community held about the world and the stories it told about itself, its collective sensibility.

Once this homogeneity begins to break down, perhaps because of a crisis of religious confidence — as seems to be the case in the sad history of Easter Island where the stone ancestors proved desperately ineffectual against a host of catastrophes — or simply through dispersal or an influx of new ideas, then the system of signs, narratives and rituals no longer fits the changing structures of belief. The forms cease to carry the religious power they once had. To our casual observer, the shaman's dance may look the same, but it has changed subtly from transubstantiation to icon; it has become dramatic metaphor.

The stories, however, remain to exert a powerful residual influence on the consciousness of the community, but now are incorporated in the kinds of productive activity we like to call art. The mythological narratives of pre-Classical Greece, for example, continued to inform the discourse of the city states long after people had stopped believing in the existence of the gods, and were eventually absorbed into the educated discourse of a wider culture to become part of the shared language of writers, painters, and musicians across Europe and beyond.

Because it is a way of making better sense of things (what has been called elsewhere, 'a way of knowing'[22]), art, like religion, is also a form of usefulness. Not because it offers us amusement, easy recognition, a way of escaping from reality — usefulness in the sense I employ it here is not to be confused with convenience or utility — but because with its religious antecedents, it helps to explain the world and to show us how we should live. When what professes to be art is not useful — when it is empty of meaning, or repetitive, or nothing more than shallow imitation — then it can no longer have a purchase on our lives.

When, on the other hand, art moves us and engages us deeply, it is because it is rooted in the sensibility of a culture to which we belong. That sensibility is itself informed by the signs and metaphors of residual belief which remain in culture as shadows, or traces, inherited by the very language we speak and through which we make ourselves understood.[23] Genuine engagement with art is thus a form of aesthetic recognition, an experience which in modern societies is as likely to disturb as confirm, illuminating paradoxes and leading us to new interpretations and greater enlightenment. Art is useful not because it is true but because it is truly edifying.

It is because drama-as-art functions in this way that a dramatic work cannot be explained, paraphrased or deconstructed into a series of essays. Like any other art form, drama is unique and non-convertible. Although plays may be interpreted by painters or composers, as in Prokofiev's *Romeo and Juliet*, for example, drama cannot be *translated* into paintings or music so that the one can be said to stand for the other. Like a primary colour in the arts spectrum, drama is reducible only to itself. Similarly, however challenging or illuminating, drama is not of necessity a means to any end, however worthy, beyond itself. It resists crassly utilitarian efforts to corral it into the service of geography, history or management training as much as it refuses to be the acquiescent servant of personal, social, or political education. In a secular age, the usefulness of drama lies in its ability to articulate meaning in particularly direct and accessible ways so that we, in turn, can make better sense of the world in which we live. For these reasons, drama is an indispensable part of the arts curriculum.

Notes and References

1 Wertenbaker, T. (1988) *Our Country's Good*, London, Methuen, Act II, scene 1.
2 Readers interested in following up these accounts should turn to Slade, P. (1954) *Child Drama*, London, University of London Press; Way, B. (1967) *Development through Drama*, London, Longman; and Davis, D. and Lawrence, C. (Eds) (1986) *Gavin Bolton: Selected Writings*, London, Longman, respectively.

3   I examine the history of this paradox in some detail in Hornbrook, D. (1989) *Education and Dramatic Art*, Oxford, Basil Blackwell, particularly in ch. 1.

4   For a classic account of this view, see Witkin, R. (1974) *The Intelligence of Feeling*, London, Heinemann.

5   See Abbs, P. (1987) *Living Powers: The Arts in Education*, London, Falmer Press, p. 55. For Abbs, the aesthetic field 'implies an intricate web of energy where the parts are seen in relationship, in a state of reciprocal flow between tradition and innovation, between form and impulse, between the society and the individual ...'

6   For some notable examples of this position, see Abbs, P. (Ed.) (1989) *The Symbolic Order*, London, Falmer Press.

7   See Hornbrook (1989) *op. cit.*, p. 63.

8   For a far more comprehensive account of the ways we characterize art than there is room for here, see Collingwood, R.G. (1958) *The Principles of Art*, Oxford, Oxford University Press.

9   Lévi-Strauss, C. (1964) *Structural Anthropology*, Harmondsworth, Allen Lane, The Penguin Press, p. 187.

10 *Ibid.*, p. 197.

11 Wittgenstein, L. (1980) *Culture and Value*, (edited by G.H. von Wright and translated by Peter Winch), Oxford, Basil Blackwell, p. 64e. Philip Larkin is less generous, describing religion in his poem 'Aubade' as, 'That vast moth-eaten musical brocade/Created to pretend we never die'. See Larkin, P. (1988) *Philip Larkin: Collected Poems* (edited by Anthony Thwaite), London, Faber and Faber.

12 Aeschylus, (1956) *The Eumenides*, ll. 828–9. (translated by Philip Vellacott), Harmondsworth, Penguin Books.

13 Geertz, C. (1983) *Local Knowledge*, New York, Basic Books, p. 97.

14 Geertz, C. (1973) *The Interpretation of Cultures*, New York, Basic Books, p. 443.

15 See Willis, P. (1990) *Common Culture*, Milton Keynes, Open University Press, p. 21.

16 *Ibid.*, p. 24.

17 See Berman, M. (1982) *All That Is Solid Melts Into Air: The Experience of Modernity*, London, Verso, p. 15. For an excel-

lent account of the modernist/post-modernist debate, see Harvey, D. (1989) *The Condition of Postmodernity*, Oxford, Basil Blackwell.

18 Pierre Bourdieu introduces the idea of 'cultural capital' in his essay 'Cultural reproduction and social reproduction' in Brown, R. (Ed.) (1973) *Knowledge, Education and Cultural Change*, London, Tavistock. Readers wishing to know more about Bourdieu's work in this field could also turn to: Bourdieu, P. and Passeron, J-C. (1990) *Reproduction in Education, Society and Culture*, (translated by Richard Nice), London, Sage.

19 Hargreaves identifies the four elements of 'conversive trauma' as follows: 'a powerful concentration of attention' (we become completely absorbed in the art object); 'a sense of revelation' (an intense feeling of heightened awareness combining recognition and profound emotional disturbance); 'inarticulateness' (we feel unable, possibly unwilling, to express the experience in words); 'an arousal of appetite' (we want the experience to be repeated). See Hargreaves, D. (1983) 'The Teaching of Art and the Art of Teaching: Towards an Alternative View of Aesthetic Learning', in Hammersley, M. and Hargreaves, A. *Curriculum Practice*, London, Falmer Press, p. 141.

20 Wittgenstein, L. (1980) *op. cit.*, p. 58e.

21 See Willis, P. (1990) *op. cit.*

22 Notably by Jerome Bruner. See Bruner, J. (1962) *On Knowing: Essays for the Left Hand*, Cambridge, MA, Harvard University Press.

23 It is what Raymond Williams has called a *structure of feeling*, that powerful sense of presence which occurs when we engage with art. As conscious holders of beliefs, we make connections with our collective sensibility and learn to know what to feel as we absorb the semiology of culture. See Wiliams, R. (1977) *Marxism and Literature*, Oxford, Oxford University Press, pp. 128–35.

Chapter 3

Telling Tales:
A Framework for Dramatic Art

Lawrence Olivier is sitting in his chair on the set of
Marathon Man. Method-schooled co-star Dustin Hoff-
man, who has been energetically preparing for his part
by undertaking gruelling training, runs up to him, ex-
hausted. 'My God, Larry,' he says, collapsing onto the
ground, 'This part will kill me.' Olivier looks at him for
a moment, and then says quietly, 'Why don't you try
acting it, dear boy?'

Apocryphal story

The Dramatic Narrative

In the previous chapter I described how the shaman of the Cuna
tribe used the story of Muu to exorcise the pain of a pregnant
woman. I proposed that the stories we tell about ourselves as a
culture or community serve not only to offer explanations and
sometimes solace but are ways of confirming our cultural identity. Stories, or narratives, in this sense are not simply entertainment (although they may be highly entertaining) but, as Roland
Barthes explains, key metaphors for the way we live our lives.

Able to be carried by articulated language, spoken or
written, fixed or moving images, gestures, and the
ordered mixture of all these substances; narrative is pre-

sent in myth, legend, fable, tale, novella, epic, history, tragedy, drama, comedy, mime, painting (think of Carpaccio's 'Saint Ursula'), stained-glass windows, cinema, comics, news item, conversation . . . it is simply there, like life itself.[1]

The mythological stories of traditional cultures are perhaps the most obvious examples of the confirmatory narrative. I have already mentioned the *Mahabharata*, the great Hindu creation myth, and the gods and goddesses of pre-Classical Greece. We could add the Chinese Taoist stories, the Innua myths of the North American Indians, the great Persian epic poem the *Shah-Nameh*, the Teutonic pantheon which inspired Richard Wagner and countless others. Many ancient stories are still enshrined in active religion, the collection which forms the Bible being an obvious example.

Sometimes, the mythical stories cultures tell are more modest. The writer Michael Rosen dicovered some while working with a class of mixed cultural origins in London. He invited his pupils to go to their parents and grandparents for stories.

Bit by bit . . . stories, songs, rhymes, proverbs and riddles began to pour out. 'Duppies' from Jamaica, demons from Hong Kong, little men from Ireland, mysterious travellers from England and unfaithful travellers from Cyprus.[2]

While some cultures regard the dramatic representation of their mythology with profound disapproval, others have extended what is often a rich oral tradition of story-telling quite naturally into drama. The Balinese Barong Dance, for example, an ancient account of the battle between Life and Death heavily influenced by the *Mahabharata* and originally enacted by priests, is now performed and kept alive by trained actors and dancers. In Europe (despite Plato's well known reservations), Greece's ancient gods and heroes drew new life from the theatre, while the early Christian Church was quick to discover the usefulness of drama in propagating New and Old Testament stories.

There are other forms of cultural dramatization too, secular in their origins yet equally powerful. Ever since Shakespeare's Henry V persuaded a ramshackle mercenary army into Harfleur with the cry 'God for Harry, England and Saint George!', nationalism has nurtured powerful stories which have received public dramatizations on and off the stage. The patriotic melodramas of the nineteenth-century London theatre, the celluloid heroics of American GIs, the 'model operas' of the Mao's Cultural Revolution; all these are forms of cultural affirmation which speak to their audiences through the medium of dramatic metaphor.

Some cultural dramatizations, however, are less immediately obvious. We have already come across one in the shape of the Balinese cockfight and seen how, in the bloody excitement of the cockfight, the Balinese dramatize facets of their own collective identity. In 1982, the world watched while a different kind of story about collective identity was played out on the stage of the South Atlantic during the Falklands Crisis. Here the scenery was bleak but real, the 'actors' died real deaths. However, as in Classical drama, for most of us the events took place off-stage and were relayed to us by messengers. Some readers will remember the redoubtable Ian McDonald, that messenger *par excellence*, whose solemn press statements brought good news and bad onto the media stage and made him quickly into a major character in the drama himself. There was tension and expectation as the story unfurled nightly before its television audience, setbacks and twists in the plot before the climax of final victory and the spectacle of 'our boys' coming home. This particular patriotic narrative, with its images of grey ships heading silently off into the mist to put an 'upstart foreigner' in his place, reassured the population of a fading world power and guaranteed its leader another prime ministerial term.[3]

Meanwhile, back in Britain, royal weddings and other state occasions continue to employ casts of thousands in the enactment of scenes from the same old imperial narrative and succeed in attracting admiring audiences beyond an impresario's wildest dreams. The elaborate way in which the British dramatize their monarchy reflects the developing importance of that institution in the metaphorical discourse of the nation.[4] Of course, this is not a phenomenon confined to Great Britain. From the Champ de Mars to Nuremburg and Red Square, dominant ideologies of left and right have told stories about themselves in the form of dramatic spectacle.

Yet there are narratives too which so pervade our daily lives that we may not even be conscious of them as such. There are the stories we tell about each other, the thumbnail biographies we use to sort and categorize our social relationships. 'Well, you know what Clare's like', we say, using what we know to be an instantly acceptable shorthand. There are the well-crafted stories we tell about ourselves, those autobiographies through which we perform acceptable versions of who we are. Erving Goffman's work on the presentation of self analyzes the way we use these narratives to manoeuvre our way through our daily encounters on the social stage.[5] Then there are apocryphal stories, such as the one about the fish that got away, and those we use to cement a social group or to exclude others. There are stories we tell about our work and about our leisure when we wish to impress, or elicit sympathy, or simply entertain.

When dramatized, all these narrative forms — mythological, religious, nationalistic, biographical, apocryphal — employ conventions such as tension, timing, humour, climax and so on to register meaning. To be successful their characters have to be instantly recognizable, their situations immediately understood. Storyteller and audience must share a common language of word, gesture and context — the narrative vocabulary which, as we saw in chapter 2, makes understanding and meaning possible in a culture. This is as true for the Ramayana as it is for *The News at Ten*, for the annual Festival of Remembrance as it is for the account we give of being stopped by the police for speeding.

Dramatized stories are integral to any cultural system. They not only reinforce a culture but also help to make it, to extend the possibility of understanding within it. Narratives of this kind not only sustain the common discourse but also subtly move it on. Dramatized stories, says Geertz, 'are not merely reflections of a pre-existing sensibility analogically presented; they are positive agents in the creation and maintenance of such a sensibility.'[6]

Whatever its formal structure, the key to a successful story, dramatized or otherwise, is that it must sustain the interest of those who listen. To do this, it must engage with the sensibility of its audience through a mutual understanding of the semiological conventions of the culture in which and for which it is enacted. Put another way, the successful dramatic narrative must be able to be 'read' by those whom it addresses. To speak of 'reading' in this sense is to acknowledge that dramatic narrative is a construction capable of interpretation and that to make sense of it we engage actively with it. The 'readers' of drama we call an audience. That there is, or will at sometime be, an audience, is implicit in the act of preparing a dramatic narrative.

Narrative, then, lies at heart of all drama, whether it be on the stage of the National Theatre or in the play-corner of the infant classroom, in an episode of *EastEnders* or an examination practical. Most often these narratives follow a conventional linear pattern; sometimes, as in performance-art, for example, or in extended classroom role-play involving a range of pedagogic tasks, the narrative structure may be highly fragmented. However simple or complex its structure, narrative is the key to understanding the special act of communication between actors and audience that we know as drama.

Establishing the Text

One way of speaking of the dramatic narrative, this piece of communication between actors and audience, is to call it a *text*.

Increasingly, the use of the word 'text' is being extended beyond the written page to describe a wide variety of readable sign systems. For social anthropologists, the study of cultures leads persuasively to the idea of regarding the manifestations of human organization as more or less readable texts.[7] In similar vein, Paul Ricoeur suggests that the meaning of human action is something which is addressed 'to an infinite number of possible "readers"', so that, 'like a text', it is always awaiting 'fresh interpretations'.[8] With such an approach we attempt to understand a cultural event like the Notting Hill Carnival not with the statistical detachment of the social scientist but by means of something more like the sensibility of the dramatic critic.

Analyses of pie-charts and histograms are displaced by inter-pretative *readings* of sign and metaphor.

In schools, pupils are most likely to come across the non-literary use of 'text' in media education. The British Film Institute's proposals for primary media education offer 'text' as a way of solving the problem of 'what word to use when you want to refer to a book and/or a film, a radio or TV program-me, a newspaper, a video, etc. all at once'.[9] Film and media teachers have become accustomed to speaking of television dis-course as a particular kind of text. (The statutory Order for English in the National Curriculum acknowledges this — students working towards level 5 in reading, for example, are required to distinguish between fact and opinion in 'non-literary and media texts'.)[10]

It is most important to understand the sense in which the word 'text' is being used here. The television 'text' is not the script, not the written words read by the announcer or per-formed by the actors, but the collection of sounds and images which we ourselves 'read' when we switch on.[11]

For this reason, reading a play in a book is not the same as reading the same play in a theatre. Attempts to 'decode' a play as it appears on the page as though it were a work of literature are likely to be unsuccessful, for to do so denies the work's origins as an active, lived event. If, instead, we regard the dramas that we make and watch as rather like television texts it is perhaps easier to accommodate the fact that dramas actually consist of spoken language, gesture, physical interaction, and so on, all of which can only be hinted at on the page. When we sit in a theatre or watch a group improvizing in the classroom we read what we see and hear much as we read what we see and hear on television (although there are significant differences which I shall come to in a moment).

By thinking of the dramatic text in this way — not as words on the page but instead as the actual performance itself — then we can see how the play in a book, or the actor's script, may be described as a way of recording what is essentially an ephemeral transaction between performers and audience; in other words, as a form of *notation*.

Already widely used by music and dance teachers, notation in drama is most obviously the record of the words said by the characters in a play together with some indication as to what they are doing — the stage directions. For some dramas (such as those performed in *commedia dell'arte*, for example) notation takes the form of a scenario. Others may have only the briefest of notated outlines, as when a teacher gives a class some pointers for an improvization. In the drama lesson, students are likely to encounter notation in the form of published plays (which they may interpret into living dramatic texts) or as they record their own work in the form of notes, scenarios or fully fledged scripts.[12]

Like the word 'music', the word 'play' can refer both to inscriptions on the page and to a living performance. Thus, the distinction between the drama itself (text) and the written record of it (notation) is most important, particularly as some plays are studied as works of literature as much, if not more, than they are performed by actors. In order to avoid confusion, I shall from now on refer to the play as it appears written down in a book as a *script*, or *playscript*. However, when using notation in drama, either to record students' ideas or as the basis for performance, we should remember that the script itself remains a literary and not a dramatic form.

The process whereby a drama, or dramatic text, is created we may call *production*. I have argued elsewhere that to describe the arts as forms of cultural production is a useful counter to de-politicized, psychological theories of arts education.[13] Here it is enough to know that production is a word already widely used in the theatre world as well as in television and by film-makers. We are all familiar with the idea of the production process as the means whereby a performance of a play is achieved.

In figure 1, we can see that the production process involves the *making* and *performing* of a dramatic text, possibly with the help of notation. This text is, in turn, received by its readers, the audience. The *reception* of the dramatic text, involving as it does both interpretation and judgment, represents the *audience response*.

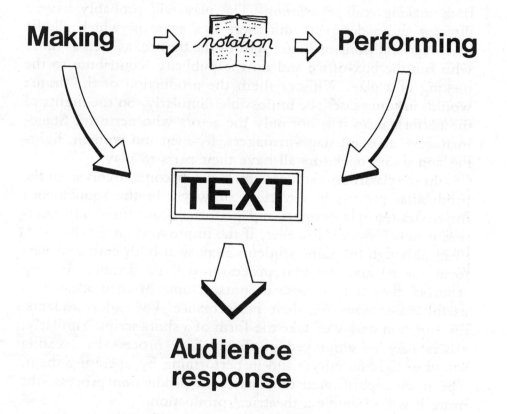

Figure 1: A framework for dramatic art.

In the theatre, the playwright is often thought of as 'making' the dramatic text. Using the model in figure 1, although the playwright may be the person who thinks up the play, his or her contribution may end at the notation stage. This is of course always true when the playwright is no longer alive. The playwright's script remains words on the page until it is realized as a living text by actors. In fact, the production process in the theatre is likely to harness the skills of many collaborators in both making and performing. The play will probably have a director and a designer, and there is a sense in which all the backstage and front-of-house staff of the theatre, as well as those who run the box-office and do the publicity, contribute to the making of a play. Without them the production of the drama would, in some cases, be impossible. Similarly, on the nights of the performances it is not only the actors who perform. Stage-managers, assistant stage-managers, fly-men and women, lighting and sound operators all have their parts to play.

In the classroom, students may also become involved in the production process in a variety of ways. In the spontaneous improvization, playwrights and performers are fused and notation is unnecessary. However, if the improvization is rehearsed, then, although the same students may well both craft and perform the drama, the two processes will be distinct. During rehearsal they may choose to notate some of their ideas as a useful *aide-mémoire* for their performance. For older students, this notation may well take the form of a short script. Similarly, others may be employed in the making process by creating sound or lighting effects and in performing by operating them. The more sophisticated the classroom production process, the more it will resemble a theatrical production.

So far I have described the process involved in the production of a live play. However, I have suggested that we daily experience many more kinds of drama than those produced in theatres or drama classrooms. My account has extended the consideration of drama to include public spectacle and the dramas of everyday life, acknowledging that we are as likely to encounter drama on the street or the screen as on the stage. All these dramatic forms may be thought of as texts. That is, they are all produced on the basis of sets of tacitly agreed cultural conventions and performed explicitly to be read and interpreted by others.

We may extend the model, therefore, to take account of three different overall categories of dramatic text. I shall call them the *stage-text*, the *electronic-text* and the *social-text*.

The stage-text is what we witness when we go to see a play in a theatre or watch a production in a drama studio, classroom, school hall, or other venue. Any dramatic performance which is live and in which the performer/audience relationship is clearly signified (by the separation of stage from auditorium, as in a traditional theatre, for example, or by the gathering of chairs in a circle in the classroom) comes into this category. School drama lessons conventionally focus on the construction of stage-texts of a particular kind — improvizations — but there are many others. The musical is one; agit-prop and street-theatre are others.

Like all texts, the stage-text employs conventions which we have learned and which can be read by its audiences. In the theatre, the 'aside' is an obvious example. A character moves out of the signified 'reality' of a scene to address the audience directly. The missing 'fourth wall' of the naturalistic stage room is another. Perhaps less obvious is the general convention that characters in a play speak in turn. Unlike real conversations which are focused on identified, contextualized listeners, stage conversations have to be read by an undifferentiated audience. Speaking in turn is an aid to intelligibility, a contrivance which we accept probably without even being aware of it. We are happy to read these conversations as 'reality' although in fact they bear little relation to the fragmentary, overlapping utterances of real everyday discourse.[14] The very structure of a stage-text, with its contrived moments of tension, its movement towards resolution, its jokes and its suspense, relies on a tacit contract about the language of convention between us as readers on the one hand, and the writer, director and performers on the other.

53

For most practical purposes we may refer to stage-texts as plays. However, because at times we will wish to make a distinction between live and televized plays, 'stage-text' remains a useful nomination.

Electronic text The electronic-text is any form of drama which has been given a degree of permanence by technological means. Unlike the stage-text, the electronic-text is (in theory, at least) infinitely reproducible. There are many forms of electronic-text which count as drama and the play is only one of them. Soap-operas, situation-comedies, feature films, commercials — I would suggest even the news (involving as it does performers, scripts and sets) — must all be included. Radio drama, as well as film and television drama, comes into this category. While the electronic-text is quite distinct from the stage-text — as we shall see, a video-recording of a student piece is by no means the same as the original performance of that piece — an electronic-text may well exist as a translation from a stage-text, as in a film of a play.

Electronic drama is, of course, a peculiarly modern phenomenon, and we should not forget that the technology which has made electronic reproduction both possible and widely accessible has vastly increased the audience for drama.[15] Any dramatic curriculum must take account of the fact that these days most students' experience of drama is gained through film and television.

Evidence of this pervasive influence surfaces everywhere in classroom improvizations. When students produce and perform dramas in the classroom they draw on a knowledge of film and television to inform their work and even the most 'authentic' tribal role-playing may owe more to the anthropologist/ adventurer Indiana Jones than we care to admit. More often, in the absence of alternative models, students will fall back on domestic settings for their improvizations, structuring their dramas as a series of short, televisual scenes, each signified perhaps by a different arrangement of chairs.[16] The naturalism inherent in this familiar format is unconsciously televisual rather than theatrical; one could say it implicitly presupposes the existence of television cameras able to pick up and follow the action from an infinite variety of positions. This may be one reason why the classroom improvization is so often visually shapeless. In the theatre, even the most naturalistic of dramas must contrive to direct itself to a spatially fixed audience. The ad hoc performance arrangements so common in classroom drama, on the other hand, with students breaking off their own work and turning round to watch from all corners of the drama room, reinforce the detachment of the performers from their audience. The danger of this quasi-televisual format is that the idea of the participating spectator can all too easily be replaced by that of the mildly curious voyeur.

Semiotic confusion between the stage-text and the electronic-text can become even more apparent when the teacher videotapes the improvization. I do not wish to disparage teachers who work in this way; a videotaped record of an improvization may serve any number of different and valuable purposes. However, if this exercise involves the camera simply being pointed at the action from a fixed position in an imaginary audience, then some confusion may arise when the tape is played back, for we are used to reading electronic-texts consisting of many different viewpoints edited together. What in fact we see is an electronic-text of a group of students making a stage-text *as if* they were making television, recorded *as if* the camera was a live audience.

Nowadays, we are all familiar with the elaborate ways in which television works at creating apparently seamless dramatic narrative. Countless 'behind the scenes' documentaries have revealed to us the armies of technicians, scene-builders, special-effects people, editors and costumiers who manufacture television 'reality' for us. The television director employs these workers to encode televisual messages which we are able to read through our learned understanding of the medium's conventions.[17] Because our exposure to these conventions is very considerable, and our understanding, as a result, very sophisticated, it is extremely difficult to make an electronic-text in the classroom which will stand the scrutiny of today's tele-visually literate students.

With the social-text we are considering those aspects of our lives which are not formally signified as dramas and yet which bear many of the characteristics of dramatic performance. The court-room, the interview, the restaurant and the wedding, the cockfight and the coronation; these are all examples of what we might call theatre analogues. We watch or participate as actors in what *seems* to be a performance and yet there is no sign above the door saying 'theatre'. Like stage and electronic- texts, the social-text too is manifest in a multitude of different ways, from the meticulously stage-managed dramas of the polity to the 1,001 significative enactments we engage in daily. The social-text is the form of what I have described elsewhere as *the dramatized society*.[18]

The social-text informs both stage and electronic-text. We engage without thinking in forms of social-text all the time and unconsciously learn to read them. The young child struggling with the spoken word will also be acquiring a complex language of gesture and nuance without which normal social intercourse would be impossible (the statutory Order for English in the National Curriculum makes reference to this under Speaking and Listening; students at level 8 are required to show 'an awareness of the contribution that facial expressions, gestures and tone of voice can make to a speaker's meaning').[19] Other customs too, like the rules which govern how close we stand to others or how we indicate that we wish to conclude a conversation — 'Well, thank you for dropping round' — will also be absorbed into a framework of highly subtle conventions. These conventions may vary considerably from culture to culture, but, without them, the highly sophisticated meaning transactions we accept without a thought would be quite impossible. Stage comedy, for example, will only work if playwright, actors and audience share this implicit vocabulary and can appreciate the spectacle of characters misreading or misusing it. Our recognition of Basil Fawlty's extreme ineptitude as both a reader of and a performer in the complex social-text of a fictional Torquay hotel is the comic basis of the television comedy *Fawlty Towers*.

How the antics of this particularly unfortunate product of English social *mores* are read by those who do not share the vocabulary is difficult to guess.[20]

In the drama lesson, the social-text is an enormously rich source for makers and readers. The accuracy with which students reconstruct and portray a social-text in the stage-text they make and perform is one indicator of their success. At the same time, the notation of social-texts in the form of accessible dramatic scripts offers further opportunities for interpretation and performance.

It is most important that students come to understand the particular conventions of these different textual forms. A mastery of this knowledge will enable students both to make effective texts themselves and to engage more deeply with those they witness. They should know, for example, that in television, a host of other 'makers' — directors, editors, vision-mixers, and so on — will mediate between the actors' performance and the final text. The television language of cut-away and close-up will be manipulated not by the performers but by those on the other side of the cameras. Stage and social-texts, on the other hand, lean more heavily on the skill of the actor to make them read. In this respect, Brecht's street–corner narrator telling the story of a road accident stands as naked before his audience as the actor playing Hamlet or the students moving into the centre of a circle of their peers to perform their improvization.[21] The actor in the electronic-text may not even witness the screening of the drama; in the stage-text and the social-text, actors and audience share both physical and temporal space as the imagined reality of the text unfolds. This in turn means that the relationship between the actor and the audience in the latter will not be one of straightforward one-way transmission. Live drama implies an interaction between performers and readers quite absent from television drama.

Education in drama should not neglect the electronic and social-text for both have an important place in the drama lesson. For one thing, the video monitor and recorder constitute an invaluable resource for examining the construction of drama of all kinds, and in some areas of the country the video monitor may be the only medium through which students may regularly experience professionally produced dramatic art.

As a different way of looking at what goes on in the drama lesson, this model of drama-as-text builds on existing practices and attempts to give them serious theoretical form. I propose it as a framework which is broad enough to incorporate all forms of drama education from the play corner to the drama school but which also takes account of the many different ways people will engage with drama during their lives. By thinking of classroom improvizations, like television dramas or street corner demonstrations, as readable texts, we are able to engage with the dramas students make in ways which acknowledge the importance not only of the producers of dramatic art but also of those who receive it — the readers of the text, the audience. All three forms of dramatic text encode the ideas of those who produce them so that they may be received and interpreted by those who watch and listen.[22]

Making, Performing and Responding

At the centre of the dramatic curriculum, I have set the idea of making and watching dramatic texts. The accessibility of the stage-text, or play, for makers, performers and audience alike, is likely to ensure its domination of educational drama practice for the foreseeable future. In view of this, from now on my attention will focus on the stage-text as the dramatic form of pre-eminent concern to drama teachers. However, we should not forget that both electronic and social-texts are also important elements of the dramatic curriculum. While they may not always be so prominent, they have nevertheless key parts to play in the structuring and teaching of dramatic art. As school drama will doubtless continue to concentrate predominantly on the producing and receiving of stage-texts, however, and as I now wish to look more closely at classroom practice, from this point in my narrative readers should assume that when I use the word 'play' I am referring to a stage-text and not, unless specifically indicated, to a television drama.

Whether it takes place in a primary classroom or a repertory theatre, the chief performers in a play are called *actors*. Through their performance, actors convey the narrative to an audience by sustaining a shared belief in the story's imagined reality. Actors, plays and audiences are thus key reference points in the dramatic curriculum.

Drama teachers have not always been accustomed to speaking of their students as actors. Instead, what goes on in the drama lesson when students perform has sometimes rather evasively been referred to as 'acting out', 'improvizing', 'taking a role' or 'portraying'. As we have seen, from Peter Slade onwards, classroom drama has tended to play down the importance of performance and the theatre language associated with it.

Yet, despite this, performances and audiences are present everywhere in classroom drama. For one thing, students seem, by and large, to enjoy being actors and watching each other perform. I am sure I am not alone in having seen groups, their arms aching in their sockets, *pleading* with the teacher, 'Can we do ours?' Most teachers are resigned to these petitions and surrender to them. However, if the dramatic curriculum experienced by the students up to that point has paid little attention to performance techniques, these 'showings' are likely to rely more on intuition and quick-wittedness than careful preparation.[23] Without clear guidance on narrative form and dramatic structure, for example, groups sent away to make improvizations will frequently spend their time in non-related activities (such as gossiping or fighting) and rely upon a rambling spontaneity when the time comes to perform. This happy-go-lucky approach to performance will be reinforced if students know that their presentations are approved in the context of what they might reveal (about a particular issue, for example) rather than for their quality as dramatic art.

The model of drama-as-text (and of improvization as a particular kind of stage-text) may help to reinstate actors and audiences as key components of the drama lesson without confirming fears that such a project will inevitably collapse into a justification of empty posturing and 'showing off'. We now need to examine how we might use this model to help us to understand and describe the processes of education in drama.

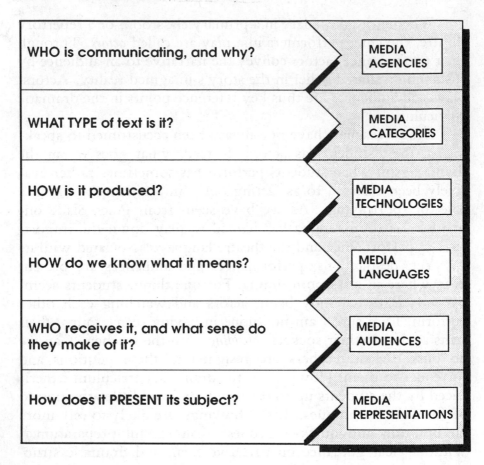

Figure 2: Signpost questions: Media education.

Primary Media Education suggests that there are a number of areas which can act as a framework for organizing the teaching of media studies. These areas can then be signposted by a series of questions, as shown in figure 2.[24] The proper concern of media teachers that students should examine carefully what they read from television and other mass media forms shapes these 'signposts' predominantly from the point of view of the recipients. However, in drama we will need to consider some 'signpost' questions for those making and performing the stage-text as well as for its audience. Figure 3 speculates how the media education questions might be reorganized and adapted for the purposes of education in drama.

FOR THOSE MAKING THE TEXT

WHAT is to be communicated and why?

> eg. We want to make a play about Ramadan to show an assembly;
> we want tell our classmates, through drama, a story we have made up;
> we want to make people aware of the problem of homelessness by making a play about it.

HOW is the subject to be presented? What type of play is it?

> eg. We will show how the festival of Eid al Fitr is celebrated in a series of short, stylised scenes linked by a narrator;
> we will enact the story, each of us taking the part of one of the characters;
> we will use a mixture of slides, recorded voices of the homeless and scripted scenes.

FOR THOSE PERFORMING THE TEXT

ARE we conveying what is intended?

> eg. We must make sure that the significance of the different elements of the festival comes across to the audience;
> our acting should be as natural as possible so that the audience thinks we really are the characters in the story;
> the audience must always be aware of the issues that lie behind the acting.

FOR THOSE RESPONDING TO THE TEXT

WHAT sense do we make of what we receive?

> eg. We learned a lot about the Eid festival but we did not always understand the conventions used by the actors;
> because some of the characters did not seem real we could not always make sense of their motivation;
> we were shocked by the images of homelessness and by the recorded statements but we were confused as to the purpose served by the acted scenes.

Figure 3: Signpost questions: Education in drama.

We have already seen how, without a performance intention, drama can easily become self-regarding and directionless. The framework in figure 3, on the other hand, shows actor and audience as entirely interdependent. Here, a dynamic actor/audience relationship — one where the narrative is carried by the actors to the audience in the spirit of the storyteller — is the basis of education in drama for both producers and recipients. As actors, students develop their craft through a growing practical experience of making communication work; as members of an audience, they watch and learn how the complex semiology of the stage mediates meaning. It is in the context of this dynamic relationship that education in drama most successfully takes place.

Starting from the question — What is to be communicated and why? — students first decide what they want to do and identify their intended audience. They then must ask themselves — How is the subject to be presented? What type of play is it? — and choose the most appropriate form of stage-text for their performance (what the film industry would call 'the treatment'). They might consider using a narrator, or choose to set the play in a circus or in the style of television quiz show. It could be that their plans are written down, notated and handed to others as a script or scenario. Eventually, they will reach a point in the production process when the key elements of the play are fixed, the scenario agreed upon and the characters sufficiently delineated for the focus to shift to preparing for the performance.

In the case where the makers of the play are also to be its performers, this is sometimes the moment when students claim they have 'finished' and are allowed to embark upon the ramshackle 'showings' to which I have already referred. In fact, the attention should now turn to getting the performance 'right' by means of practice and repetition. The idea of rehearsal is no less important for drama than it is for any other performing art. Few musicians or dancers would think of performing without adequate preparation, and that will normally mean going over a piece many times. As rehearsals proceed, students should be continually asking — Are we conveying what is intended? Finally, when they judge themselves adequately prepared, the student actors join with the other elements of the text — the spoken language, the gesture, the scenery, the music — in the performance itself.

Finally, the play will be received by an audience whose members will ask of themselves — What sense do we make of what we receive? Meaning will be implicit in every move the actors make, each change of intonation, every glance. Those watching will probably respond to the play partly by reading the drama as everyday life. That is, they will interpret what they see and hear as a reproduction of a social-text, particularly if the work is naturalistic in form. So finely tuned are our interpretative faculties to the social-texts we read every day that the raising of an eyebrow can transform our interpretation of an action while the slightest variation in the length of a pause can signify to us a completely different state in the relationship between two characters. However, at the same time as the members of the audience are reading the social signifiers embedded in the text, they will also be aware that they are being told a story, that although what they are watching is in the present tense, it is not in fact the reality it signifies. They will thus also bring to bear on what they read a learned vocabulary of dramatic conventions. Knowledge of this vocabulary will allow the watchers to read into the most minimal signifiers whole imaginative worlds. They will accept a painted tree for a forest, an actor grasping her collar with an upward grimace for a shower of rain, a top hat for capitalism, a simple raised platform for the vasty fields of France. The success of the performers and of the stage-text produced by the students might be measured by the extent to which all this signification is the result of intention as opposed to accident.

To summarize, the story, or narrative, is at the heart of drama. Dramatized stories of all kinds pervade our lives, many standing as key metaphors through which we make sense of the world. For us to be able to 'read' these stories successfully, there must be an agreement about meaning shared by storytellers and audience — a common dramatic language. This language will extend beyond the spoken word to embrace a range of different dramatic signifiers.

Borrowing from media education, I have proposed that we call these dramatic narratives texts. The dramatic text is another way of thinking of the play in performance (if we write down what the characters say in the form of a script, we are notating the drama). There are three kinds of dramatic text we need to consider in drama education — the stage-text, the electronic-text and the social-text. Making any dramatic text is a form of cultural production, quite possibly involving many kinds of cultural worker. However, the chief performers of the dramatic text are called actors; its readers are members of an audience. Actors, texts and audiences are thus intrinsic to dramatic art.

In the drama classroom, students will spend most of their time making and responding to stage-texts or plays. Education in drama happens in the production process, where students make and perform texts, and in the reception process, where they become critical witnesses. In this way, a simple progression from intention, through making and performing to audience response is both the basis of dramatic story-telling and the framework we need for education in drama. By characterizing dramatic art as essentially a matter of making, performing and responding to plays, the structures proposed here give shape to the 'practical artistic subject' identified by HMI.[25] How the framework for dramatic art translates into classroom practice will be the subject of the following chapters.

Notes and References

1   Barthes, R. (1977) 'Introduction to the structural analysis of narratives', in *Image — Music — Text*, London, Fontana, p. 79. It is interesting that Robert Watson has also chosen this quotation from Roland Barthes in his contribution (1990) to this series, *Film and Television in Education*, London, Falmer Press.

2   Rosen, M. (1990) 'Script for Action', in *The Times Educational Supplement*, 27 April.

3   For a sharp account of the media representation of the Falklands War (and Ian McDonald's role in it), see Harris,

R. (1983) *Gotcha! The Media, the Government and the Falklands Crisis*, London, Faber and Faber.

4   So accustomed have we become to the slick, adulatory royal dramas of post war years that it is easy to forget that these are a relatively recent innovation. According to David Cannadine, Queen Victoria's coronation 'was completely unrehearsed; the clergy lost their place in the order of the service; the choir was pitifully inadequate; the Archbishop of Canterbury put the ring on a finger that was too big for it; and two of the trainbearers talked throughout the entire ceremony'. Cannadine, D. (1983) 'The Context, performance and meaning of Ritual: The British Monarchy and the "Invention of Tradition", c. 1820–1977', in Hobsbawn, E. and Ranger, T. (Eds) *The Invention of Tradition*, Cambridge, England, Cambridge University Press, p. 118.

5   See Goffman, E. (1969) *The Presentation of Self in Everyday Life*, Harmondsworth, Penguin Books.

6   Geertz, C. (1973) *The Interpretation of Cultures*, New York, Basic Books, p. 451.

7   'The *interpretatio naturae* of the middle ages, which culminating in Spinoza, attempted to read nature as Scripture, the Nietzschean effort to treat value systems as glosses on the will to power (or the Marxian one to treat them as glosses on property relations), and the Freudian replacement of the enigmatic text of the manifest dream with the plain one of the latent, all offer precedents, if not equally recommendable ones' *ibid.*, p. 449.

8   Ricoeur, P. (1981) *Hermeneutics and the Human Sciences*, Cambridge, England, Cambridge University Press, p. 208.

9   Bazalgette, C. (Ed.) (1989) *Primary Media Education: A Curriculum Statement*, London, British Film Institute, p. 5.

10   Department of Education and Science (1990a) *English in the National Curriculum (Statutory Order for English)*, HMSO.

11   According to Fiske and Hartley, any attempt 'to decode a television "text" as though it were a literary text is ... doomed to failure ... its "logic" is oral and visual'. Fiske, J. and Hartley, J. (1978) *Reading Television*, London, Methuen, p. 14.

12   As Jonathan Miller points out, the notation of drama is a far less precise affair than that of music. There are just too many variables. See Miller, J. (1986) *Subsequent Performances*, London, Faber and Faber, pp. 38–48.

13   See Hornbrook, D. (1989) *Education and Dramatic Art*, Oxford, Basil Blackwell, ch. 9.

14   Directing Chekhov, Jonathan Miller challenged this convention by encouraging actors to remember the idioms of normal conversation. 'On the page, we see the meaning of what is heard and not what is *actually* heard … In a strange way, if you want to make the speeches seem real you have to overlook the way in which they are written down and try to remember how people actually sound …' Miller, J. (1986) *op. cit.*, p. 168.

15   See Benjamin, W. (1970) 'The Work of Art in the Age of Mechanical Reproduction', in *Illuminations*, London, Fontana/Collins.

16   This trend is not peculiar to the drama lesson. The episodic style of many contemporary playwrights suggests that they too have been influenced by television in this way.

17   This understanding is becoming ever more sophisticated. The famous 'wobble-dissolve', for instance, once the required signifier of the rapid passing of time in films now looks simply old-fashioned. A straight cut from present to past can be read quite satisfactorily without resort to what now seems an unnecessarily cumbersome device.

18   See 'The Dramatized Society', in Hornbrook, D. (1989), *op. cit.*, ch. 10. Examples of the infiltration of our discourse by the language of the theatre are plentiful. A supermarket recently put up a sign over the door through which its staff had to pass in order to enter the store. It read, 'REMEMBER, you are about to go on stage'. In similar vein, here is a quotation from the up-market magazine, *Period Living*: 'Creating a period feel in a room is like creating a theatrical set. It is essential to obtain the right props and then arrange them so that they can speak for themselves.' See also Goffman (1969) *op. cit.*

19   Department of Education and Science (1990a) *op. cit.*

20   For how long it will be possible to make the assumption

that *everyone* has seen *Fawlty Towers*, I do not know. Since the series was first broadcast in 1975 there have been countless repeat showings and videotapes of all twelve episodes are on sale throughout Great Britain.

21 Those not familiar with Brecht's comparison of epic theatre with the account of an accident given by a passer-by, should turn to 'The Street Scene — A Basic Model for an Epic Theatre', in Brecht, B. (1964) *Brecht on Theatre: The Development of an Aesthetic* (edited and translated by John Willett), New York, Hill and Wang.

22 That is not to say that the dramatic text is a puzzle to be decoded in order that its maker's real ideas may be revealed. The search for elusive authorial intention is one of the more fruitless enterprises of literary theory. What the dramatic text expresses is unique to the text itself and to the multiple interpretations of its audience.

23 For an all too recognizable account of a nightmare lesson of this kind, see Watkins, B. (1981) *Drama and Education*, London, Batsford, pp. 64–6. Also quoted in Hornbrook, D. (1989), *op. cit.*, pp. 144–6.

24 Bazalgette, C. (1989) *op. cit.*, p. 8.

25 See Department of Education and Science (1989b) *Drama from 5 to 16: HMI Curriculum Matters 17*, HMSO, p. 1.

Chapter 4

The Dramatic Curriculum 1: Production

Poetry is manufacture. A very difficult, very complex kind, but a manufacture ... You mustn't make the manufacturing, the so-called technical process, an end in itself. But it is this process of manufacture that makes the poetic work fit for use.

Vladimir Mayakovsky, 1926[1]

Work in Progress

The history of drama-in-education has seen the teacher in many roles. From Harriet Finlay-Johnson's pre-Great War advocacy of teachers as 'fellow-workers, friends and playmates' to Peter Slade's 'loving allies' and the 'teacher/facilitator' of dramatic pedagogy, the drama teacher has variously joined in with and stood aside from the making of plays in the classroom.[2] For all their differences, these approaches share progressive education's traditional ambiguity towards the transmission of skills and knowledge and to the question of critical intervention in students' work. While Peter Slade was content to remain on the sidelines, simply drawing a group's attention to 'some little piece of beauty they may have missed',[3] unabashed interventionists, like Dorothy Heathcote, tended to restrict their post-operative comments to what they identified as the drama's hidden lessons. Either way, skills in and knowledge about drama itself were acquired only incidentally by the participants and the aesthetic outcome, the dramatic product, tended to remain beyond the critical realm.

While these ways of working have sometimes led to good drama teachers becoming most impressive classroom practitioners, they place upon the drama specialist quite unique demands in terms of the conduct of the drama lesson. Like other solo performers, drama teachers labour long and hard to gain the commitment of their audiences (this may be one reason why factors like 'involvement' rate so highly in drama assessment schemes), and although this effort can sometimes lead to educational bonds developing between teacher and taught in drama not found anywhere else in the school, such special relationships are extremely exacting of a teacher's emotional energy.

In the secondary school, for example, there is often an implicit expectation that the drama specialist should perform as a kind of 'master (or mistress) of the revels'. Put another way, I might say that as a secondary student in drama I expect my interest to be continually stimulated. Indeed, I might well see the drama lesson as pre-eminently a time when the teacher uses his or her skills to keep me amused. I look forward to a new stimulus each week, and I resent having to recall whatever it was we did the week before. I expect lots of things to do which are self-contained and satisfying in themselves and which I can happily forget about when the lesson is over. In drama, I seek the kind of instant gratification I get from PE or games. In the secondary school staff-room, one need go no further for evidence to support this perception than the daily cover list. Drama must surely be top of the non-specialist's list of 'subjects for which I would least like to lose my free period'. Despite valiant efforts on the part of conscientious drama colleagues, it remains very difficult to 'set work' for drama which can be adequately supervised by the non-specialist.

The model of the drama teacher as guarantor of a never-ending supply of stimulating classroom experiences is not only an exhausting one but also imprisons the teacher in a cycle of continuous gratification which makes the actual *teaching* of drama very difficult. The strong emphasis which has traditionally been placed on process in drama — expressive, developmental or pedagogic — and the corresponding conceptual invisibility of the dramatic product, lies at the root of this problem, for it has obscured the idea of drama as craft.[4]

For teachers in the other arts disciplines, describing elements of what they do as induction into a craft, would not, I suspect, be seen as antipathetic to a process model of arts education. In visual art the teacher will find ways of developing skill with clay, or the ability to use paints and no musician or dancer would deny the importance of technique. Yet, in schools, drama lacks any really systematic approach to its craft, with the result that it is often difficult to trace success in drama (as a performer, for example) back to any identifiable educational programme at either primary or secondary levels.[5]

It was also said by some in the 1980s that drama was unique because it had no subject-specific body of knowledge. For these proponents of drama–as–methodology, what you came to know through drama was limited only by the limits of human knowledge itself.[6] This is partly true. To predict what anyone will learn as a result of engagement with art is, of course, impossible. However, the proposition that drama itself has no epistemological basis is only sustainable if you are prepared to reserve the word 'drama' for certain highly specialized classroom practices. In fact, as we have seen, drama mediates meaning through a complex system of signifiers — it has its own semiology. This semiology has also a history; as the culture of which it is part becomes more diverse so the semiology of drama becomes richer and more complex. By isolating drama–in–education from the wider discourse of the arts world we conceal from young people the forms of skills and knowledge which allow them to participate in a dramatic culture, for participation in a dramatic culture means being able to read its conventions and manipulate its forms. This may involve watching a play or taking part in a class production, but it also may mean getting a job as a stage electrician, or as a theatre administrator, or as an actor. These, and countless other forms of engagement with dramatic art, require specific forms of dramatic knowledge and understanding.

Another major weakness of the expressive, developmental and pedagogic models which dominated practice for so long was that they had no conceptual means of addressing fundamental questions of quality and achievement.[7] The acquisition of any craft and the knowledge that goes with it, requires practice, repetition, self-criticism and direction. These processes are only tolerable if motivated by a strong desire to progress, to become more proficient, to know more. In the past, the absence from the classroom of systematic approaches to critical analysis or shared criteria for the assessment of dramatic product often made it difficult for students to identify in drama any concept of *progression*. For many, I suspect, how they might have set about getting *better* at drama remained a mystery.

By using the framework of making, performing and responding to plays proposed in the previous chapter we should be able to find ways of building a dramatic curriculum which places the emphasis on the productive, cultural and aesthetic character of drama as opposed to its therapeutic or pedagogic utility and within which it is possible to identify clear routes of progression. From this sure foundation would then grow related practices covering all the skills, knowledge and creative opportunities we associate with the art of drama. Within such a conceptual structure students may expect to progress as designers and directors as well as playwrights and performers and to develop their judgment and skills of interpretation as well as their ability to devise and perform.[8]

A further advantage of this eclectic programme is that it may help to draw back to drama those students whose shyness has led to low scores on the 'group participation' scale. As things stand, any reluctance to 'muck in' with the others can all too easily count as failure in drama.[9] The fact is, some young people would actually *rather* work the tape-recorder or operate the lighting than join in an improvization. Many, given the chance, would accomplish these tasks rather well, and might even, as a result, develop a life-long interest in the theatre. A girl who squirms with embarrassment at the thought of being asked to improvize may turn out to be an acute observer and potentially talented director. A boy who rarely speaks may have an eye for design or an ear for dialogue. For some, the pleasure of watching drama may far surpass that of participating in it. The dramatic curriculum in schools must allow for all these interests.

When it comes to identifying practical strategies for the

development of the dramatic curriculum, the tenacity of the 'plays in small groups' model of the drama lesson, to which passing reference has already been made, suggests that it may have greater potential than some of its detractors admit. Perhaps in the past the problem has been not so much with the model itself but in the realizing of this potential within the existing conceptual apparatus of drama-in-education. Without an adequate theory of audience, and by implication, of performance, small group play making would always have remained an emasculated practice, and teachers would have continued to be frustrated by the paucity of its outcomes. In fact, its popularity among students is in large measure due to the expectation of performance, and it is that same heady combination of trepidation and excitement that draws young people to youth theatre or the school play that drives the production process forward in the classroom.

It is around this core motivating activity that the dramatic curriculum will develop. Under it, a visit to the drama classroom will no longer reveal the teacher/motivator in action with the latest drama game or exercise but a multiplicity of examples of independent learning. The atmosphere may be similar to that in art with students engaged in a variety of activities related to the production process. Rehearsal may be only one of these, for countless other tasks must be completed if the production is to be successful. Here the teacher is giving advice to one group, directing another, teaching another how to use four lanterns on stands to best effect. On occasions the whole class will come together for a formal session on acting technique or design, or to see how one group's play is progressing or to share ideas.

An idealistic picture, perhaps. However, most students do enjoy participating in some way in drama. What de-motivates them is the thought that their work is aimless and the lack of any real sense of achievement from what they do. A rambling succession of unrelated drama activities, however energetically presented, is calculated to have precisely this effect over time. By proposing instead a practice-based dramatic curriculum with clear strategies for progression it will be possible to build on drama's formidable strengths as a motivating force without requiring of hard-pressed teachers an endless bill of quick-fix drama acts.

A Framework for Making and Performing Plays

Production in drama — making and performing plays — is comparable with composing and performing in music, choreographing and performing in dance. The production process begins with an idea and ends (possibly) with a performance. For play makers, like film makers, the script (if there is one) is only one element of the process, the actors only one kind of participant in the crafting of the final text.

Translated into schools, production in drama will take a variety of forms. Some activities, such as the school play, may mirror the professional theatre; others, probably most, will be experimental and exploratory with clearly defined educational ends. However, all will share, with differing emphases, the same fundamental structure; all will have as their goal, the production of a stage-text or play.

The actual processes involved in making and performing plays are interrelated and complex. However, figure 4 shows how the production process in drama may, for clarification, be broken down under a series of headings. These headings, together with some examples of accompanying practice, indicate how we might make sense of what happens when students come together to make and perform plays.

Investigating — Is the Idea Viable?

Investigation is the first stage in the production process, that is, where the idea for a play germinates. For the professional playwright, the process of investigating may involve thinking up the characters, inventing a plausible story and wondering if the combination will work as a drama.

In the classroom, the investigating process is often stimulated by the teacher. At primary level, the stimulus may come in

Figure 4: Production.

the form of a question, such as: 'How do you think the people living there would have reacted when Christopher Columbus first stepped ashore in the Bahamas? Imagine what that meeting might have been like and see if you can make up a play about it to show us.' Later, in the secondary school, the teacher may pose a series of questions, relating to a topical social issue for example, and ask groups to investigate how they think their views might be represented dramatically.

On the other hand, it may be that the idea for a play comes from the students themselves. A primary classroom topic might inspire a group to make up a play; a theme from television or from their own experience may stimulate a group of secondary students to investigate its dramatic potential.

However, we should not forget that the idea for a play may also come from a published script. I have seen a primary class so excited by extracts from *A Midsummer Night's Dream* that their enthusiasm led to a full-scale production of the play. While for some, such a project may be somewhat on the ambitious side, scripts are nevertheless an invaluable source of inspiration at all ages. Students may well enjoy reading a play and wish to investigate how it might be realized as a living text.

The investigating stage, which starts with an idea, may get no further. The idea may be rejected. However, if the investigation suggests that there is a play to be made, then the process of experimentation begins.

Experimenting — Trying Out Ideas

The playwright will now start to write, or as I would rather put it, *notate* the play. The original idea will crystallize into words on a page. These words will be either those later to be spoken by the characters or indicators as to how they should move. Usually, scenes will be written and re-written many times before this process of experimentation is concluded.

Meanwhile, our students with the Columbus story are trying out ways of showing the momentous first recorded meeting between Europe and the Americas. Important decisions have to be made. What language do the islanders speak? Not English, surely? But then Columbus wasn't English-speaking either. What should we wear? More investigating needed here; the children may well go back to the teacher or to the class library for information. As every primary teacher knows, drama is a powerful motivation for learning. These young playwrights will probably not choose to notate what they do. Instead, they will experiment in action, trying and re-trying scenes until they are satisfied that the story is right.

At secondary level, the initial stages of the production process may be different. We might imagine a class of key stage 3 students in an inner-city comprehensive school reading Elyse Dodgson's play about the experiences of Commonwealth immigrants in the 1950s, *Motherland*.[10] Some of the 14-year-olds hear echoes in the play of the stories their grandparents tell and want to act out some of the scenes. They begin to experiment with different ways of bringing the script to life.

Meanwhile, some key stage 4 students from a drama option group in the same school are experimenting with ideas about advertising. They have watched a documentary about television commercials and want to incorporate a television monitor into their drama. They are trying out a range of different dramatic structures which will make this possible. To help them, the teacher has introduced them to some of the mixed-media devices used by Erwin Piscator in the 1920s. This time, almost certainly, some form of notation will be necessary, as the play will lean heavily on accurate timing and the integration of effects. However, these 15 and 16-year-old students wish to explore a range of possibilities before committing themselves to a written scenario.

Designing — Shaping the Play

By now, the playwright will have handed the script to the director and designer of the play. From this point, although alterations may still be made to the original notation, the director and the designer will lead a production team which will eventually realize the playwright's ideas. Their job is to visualize the play in performance and to guide the actors and scene-builders through the production process. Because the play-wright's notation provides only an indication of the final living text (much less comprehensive than the musician's score) then the task of realizing it is one of collective interpretation.

Our primary school production team faces a similar task, although without the same demarcation of roles. In this little 'theatre collective', each member of the group may have a say on every aspect of the production process.[11] In practice, experience suggests that questions of design are likely to be a low priority — costumes, if any, will be rudimentary and the playing space whatever there is to hand. Left to their own devices there will be a consciousness that they want the play to look right for an audience but very much less certainty as to how this might be achieved. If this is the case, the teacher should not be afraid to suggest ideas.

The *Motherland* group will be facing design problems of a different kind. For one thing, as with most scripts, the extremely imprecise nature of the dramatic notation the students have before them will allow for many different interpretations of the movement and spacing of characters. Also, although the script gives little indication of the setting, the spatial limits of the playing area must be defined and decisions made about scenery and properties. These fundamental design questions are raised immediately when the students embark upon an interpretation. The devised piece about advertising will be forced, by its technology if nothing else, to be careful about positioning, setting and lighting. The presence of a television monitor cannot but affect the shaping of the performance that goes on around it.

Teacher intervention can be particularly useful at this stage. Students will usually need no encouragement to investigate and experiment, but the process of translating their ideas into an effective piece of drama capable of being read by others is a sophisticated one; they will need help at all levels. Improvization of the kind familiar to drama teachers is a useful part of the play making process. However, it has an inward focus which discourages students from paying attention to the perceptions of a possible audience. The teacher, in the early stages possibly the only audience for the work, should use this external perspective to help students learn about the importance of how a play looks. Certainly, information and ideas about design should be available to the Columbus play makers and the *Motherland* group; the teacher should not be deterred from stepping in to show the effects of different settings or stage arrangements. As with any art form, some things in drama simply have to be taught.

In the secondary school, it might well be appropriate for design to become the special project of an individual or a group of students. Once the basic structure of the text has been established and agreed upon, then responsibility for the setting and other design aspects of the play, however simple, would provide a valuable learning experience. After all, drama is not just about performing, and students should understand the importance of the contribution made by other participants in the production process.

Directing — Making the Play Work

Although in the professional theatre every director has a particular style, the role of the director in relation to the cast and other members of the production team is, by convention, well established. When the teacher directs the school play, this essentially hierarchical relationship transfers to a school setting. In some cases this is appropriate — the good teacher/director can draw achievement in drama from young people with the lowest of expectations.

In the drama classroom, however, the model of the authoritarian director is frowned upon for understandable reasons. Those in the Columbus group will fight their battles among themselves and, with a little nudging maybe, achieve a final victory as they perform before their friends. No wonder that drama has for so long been seen to have a role in fostering positive group dynamics. However, the question that must be asked is this: while acknowledging their *social* achievement, have the children learned as much about *drama* as they might have done with sympathetic external direction?

There is no simple answer to this question, but it is important to realize that a strategy of non-intervention does not always result in the most productive learning. It must not be assumed that completely democratic group devising is the most educative way of working nor that it necessarily produces the best results. With older groups, there is a powerful argument for allowing the student with some facility as a director to exercise this skill for the benefit of the group as a whole. In school, directing should be seen as simply another facet of the production process, and not as a matter of status.

Above all, when it comes to directing in the classroom, it is important to distinguish between the production process as an opportunity for the exercise of group democracy and the production process as differentiated collaboration towards essentially dramatic ends. Neither approach necessarily excludes the other, but the teacher must be clear about where he or she wishes to place the emphasis. With the director such a prominent figure in today's theatre, ways have clearly to be found of giving students some experience of directing if the eclectic aims of dramatic art are to be fulfilled.[12]

Editing — Getting the Play Right

To find an analogy in the professional field, I shall leave the theatre for a moment and instead turn to the processes of film making. In film and television, editing is the process whereby all the pieces that have been made and recorded are juggled about until it is judged that they read satisfactorily. A key part of this process is the viewing of a variety of possible alternatives, or 'rough-cuts'.

School drama's traditional emphasis on spontaneity and its long history of non-intervention has meant that any critical analysis is likely to be conducted at a post-production stage. In these circumstances, comments from the teacher and other members of the class, however constructive and useful, are retrospective, coming too late for alterations to the text to be made. It is intended that account will be taken of them in the next piece of work. A practice where students first make 'rough-cuts' of their work to present to the class, on the other hand, admits critical interpretation from outside at a point when changes are still possible. We can identify parallels in other areas of arts education: the way in which the art teacher comments constructively on a student's painting while it is still on the easel, for example, or the advice given to groups engaged in composition or in the choreographing of a dance. Editing in the drama classroom is a way of testing an audience's reading of a piece in preparation.

A further aspect of editing which makes it such a useful educational device, is the way in which it also sharpens the perceptions of the classroom audience. Whereas during post-production analysis students can speculate as to how a drama might have been, here those suggestions can actually be put to the test. Advice offered on a scene, or on a piece of characterization, can be incorporated in the next 'rough-cut' and further judgment made. Editing is not only a way of constructive intervention in students' 'work in progress' but also a means of developing increasingly sophisticated forms of audience response.

There is a danger, of course, that the production of too many 'rough-cuts' may quench students' enthusiasm for a piece; the balance between spontaneity and revision must be carefully judged by the teacher. For younger children, such as those engaged on the Columbus play, one pre-performance viewing might be appropriate. Even that preliminary, however, can help to sharpen up the final presentation and stimulate a more committed and perceptive audience response.

The *Motherland* group will probably require the mediating presence of the teacher as a range of interpretations are pasted together for critical viewing. For the 15 and 16-year-olds in the drama option class, editing should have become an accepted part of the production process. At this level, students should be able to call upon others in the class independently of the teacher as and when the need arises for judgment on alternative texts. For all three groups, editing gives students the opportunity to evaluate how their texts are being read and to make changes accordingly.

Rehearsing — Fixing the Play

As the professional actor begins rehearsals, certain elements of the production are likely already to be in place. The play will have been cast and copies of the script (perhaps subject to minor alterations) will be in the actors' hands. The designer will have produced a model of the set, the date of the first performance will have been fixed. In varying degrees, the director will know how the play will look and where the actors will move on the stage. Although usually there will still be opportunities to contribute suggestions, rehearsals are traditionally where the actors use their skills to realize the ideas of the playwright and the director.[13]

The educational and collaborative nature of classroom drama make this 'transmission' model less than appropriate. However, there may be something to be learned from the disciplines imposed by the professional rehearsal. As I have already pointed out, the danger with classroom play making is that once the ideas have been agreed upon, then the urge to proceed to performance without further ado is sometimes difficult to resist. Unfortunately, cries of, 'We've finished ours, Miss', can often be an indication of boredom resulting from a failure to understand that any more remains to be done, rather than performance readiness.

In the school context, rehearsal must allow scope for changes in the text but should focus on the need to make the play reproducible. Although little or nothing may be notated, what is finally presented should not be reliant upon the off-the-cuff spontaneity of the performers but should be the result of careful crafting and preparation. Students must learn that a successful drama is rarely the result of intuitive accident but comes about through a process of considered choices supported by disciplined practice. (In this respect, role-play, relying as it does on the unrehearsed responses of the participants, might be said to be the antithesis of serious play making.)[14]

An important task of the drama teacher is making students understand the importance of rehearsal. The editing process is helpful here; inadequate preparation will often reveal itself at the 'rough-cut' stage. However, the fact remains that any move away from the spontaneous will mean the drama teacher coming to share with the instrumental music tutor the problem of persuading students to practice.

Two factors help here. First, the high level of commitment to their work, which has always been a characteristic of students involved in drama, will make the drive to 'get it right' a powerful one. Low expectations on the part of the teacher will mean students will be able to 'get it right' with minimal effort. Careful preparation will seem pointless. The higher the expectation of the class and the teacher, the more rigorously students will need to rehearse. Second, the promise of performance at a specified future date will act as a strong stimulus for energetic preparation, particularly if the occasion is suitably formal (with another class or a school assembly as audience, for example). No one who has ever directed a school play could doubt the productive force of a performance deadline.

All three of our examples will need rehearsal. The young performers in the Columbus play might benefit from the spur of performance to another class. A promise to show *Motherland* to some of those women who lived through the experiences described in the play would raise the play makers' own self esteem and give a particularly keen edge to 'getting it right'. The piece on advertising could stand a lunch-time school audience, perhaps, or may already be destined for the adjudication of an examiner.

Of course, carrots of these kinds are not the whole answer. Once again, the teacher has to use his or her skills to strike the balance between the students' enthusiasm for a project (without which it stands no chance of success) and the often repetitive tasks involved in making it work.

Managing — Organizing the Play

The technical rehearsal, or 'tech', is a familiar pre-performance ritual in the professional theatre, almost the last part of the play making process. Actors go through their entrances and exits, 'topping and tailing' scenes, and for the first and only time the sailors are exaggerated, reconstructed from an islander perception with materials likely to have been available to them after the ships' departure.

The text itself is made up of a mixture of scripted speech and improvisation. With the help of the teacher, the students have built a rhythmic beat into the narrator's lines (they looked at sections of Longfellow's *Hiawatha* as part of their investigation) to give the narration a more formal quality. There are five students speaking short sections of the narration, and they have all learned their lines. The scenes of confrontation, in which all the other students are involved, are improvized within an agreed scenario, the students using their own natural modes of discourse in their attempts to understand the intruders' gobbledygook. There is much use of gesture for the group has learned about the importance of non-verbal language. They use simple percussion to punctuate events and to indicate a change of scene or the passage of time.

The notated scenario with the sections of scripted narration forms a secure structure for performance. The students are clear at all times as to what they should do, and although the improvized scenes change and develop each time they are played, like the actors in the *commedia*, the scenario ensures that the students always know where a scene starts and where it must end. This format gives scope for the creativity of the students — it is they who have devised the piece — while providing, under the guidance of the teacher, an effective dramatic framework within which that creativity may be expressed.

That evening the lights go down on the invited audience gathered for the *Motherland* performance. Parents and grandparents who disembarked in England from the West Indies in the 1950s have come to hear their story told by a new generation. The lights go up on the central playing area, the music plays out and the story begins. Thoughtful interpretation of the original script backed up by meticulous rehearsing results in a powerful presentation. Here, the script and its notated cueing provide a more detailed framework than the Columbus scenario. However, there is no doubt that the performance has been the students' own. Sensitive characterization has fleshed out the thin traces of personality indicated by the written lines and the

hidden performers — stage-managers and technical operators — have centre stage. It is a last chance to get cues sorted out and for effects to be integrated with the actors' performances. However, the organization of a successful theatrical production extends beyond the stage to the auditorium — 'front-of-house' — and to the whole administrative support system upon which the play relies.

Only the most elaborate school production is likely to need administration based on the professional model. Even the presentation of a simple piece in the classroom, however, requires careful management if it is to achieve its maximum effect. Such matters as ensuring actors enter on cue, that their props are where they should be, that the audience knows when the play has begun; all will require attention if the creative work generated through the production process is to be sympathetically presented. Few things are more disappointing than a potentially powerful drama ruined by scrappy presentation.

As every stage-manager knows, a good prompt book is at the heart of a successfully organized performance. Alongside the final version of the playwright's script are listed all the actors' moves and the lighting and sound cues. The prompt book represents another stage in the notation process, the most complete attempt that will be made to establish a written record of a live performance. In schools, the prompt book is rare. Even the school play may rely for its cues upon a few scribbles in the margin of a script or on the memories of individual actors and backstage helpers. For dramatic art, however, the prompt book and the disciplines associated with it, are an essential part of good practice.

Take, for example, our *Motherland* group. The students have decided to perform some scenes from the play in the school drama studio. They have chosen an acting area in the centre of the floor and have lit it with four pairs of lanterns on stands. The students wish to introduce the play with music. How is this to be integrated in the opening of the performance? What they want to achieve will require the coordination of a number of performers: the sound and lighting operators, the person letting the audience in and the actors.

hidden performers — stage-managers and technical operators — have centre stage. It is a last chance to get cues sorted out and for effects to be integrated with the actors' performances. However, the organization of a successful theatrical production extends beyond the stage to the auditorium — 'front-of-house' — and to the whole administrative support system upon which the play relies.

Only the most elaborate school production is likely to need administration based on the professional model. Even the presentation of a simple piece in the classroom, however, requires careful management if it is to achieve its maximum effect. Such matters as ensuring actors enter on cue, that their props are where they should be, that the audience knows when the play has begun; all will require attention if the creative work generated through the production process is to be sympathetically presented. Few things are more disappointing than a potentially powerful drama ruined by scrappy presentation.

As every stage-manager knows, a good prompt book is at the heart of a successfully organized performance. Alongside the final version of the playwright's script are listed all the actors' moves and the lighting and sound cues. The prompt book represents another stage in the notation process, the most complete attempt that will be made to establish a written record of a live performance. In schools, the prompt book is rare. Even the school play may rely for its cues upon a few scribbles in the margin of a script or on the memories of individual actors and backstage helpers. For dramatic art, however, the prompt book and the disciplines associated with it, are an essential part of good practice.

Take, for example, our *Motherland* group. The students have decided to perform some scenes from the play in the school drama studio. They have chosen an acting area in the centre of the floor and have lit it with four pairs of lanterns on stands. The students wish to introduce the play with music. How is this to be integrated in the opening of the performance? What they want to achieve will require the coordination of a number of performers: the sound and lighting operators, the person letting the audience in and the actors.

All decisions about such matters are notated in the form of instructions in the special copy of the script called the prompt book. The student who has kept these notes up-to-date during the rehearsal and who will cue the others, is, of course, that key player, the stage-manager. The others who will also have essential non-acting roles to play during the performance are the two technical operators and the steward or front-of-house (FOH) manager. The technical rehearsal will involve all these hidden performers (although in the *Motherland* play, the FOH manager will be the teacher). The group knows that getting the technical cues right and the sound and lighting at the correct levels is every bit as important as remembering lines and acting cues.

For some, this may all seem rather excessive. However, I regard the care and attention taken over these details as a mark of respect for students' work, equivalent to the careful framing by the art teacher of a student's painting. Blu-tack and drawing pins may be adequate for work-in-progress but not for the exhibition.

So how is the primary group approaching the management of their performance? The Columbus play is to be performed as part of junior assembly. The school's hall has no blackout and no stage lights. The students are not using any recorded sound. What is important is that the play should be incorporated within the structure of the assembly and that the students should know where to wait and when to come on. The four short scenes which make up the story are to be linked by a narration. The arrangements for this and for the changes of scene covered by it must be organized and rehearsed. The prompt book consists of sheets of sugar paper pasted up on the sides of the stage which remind students of their cues. The stage-manager has the responsibility for checking these and making sure everyone knows what they should do and that they are all in their places. This important role has been entrusted to a volunteer from the group who also has a small acting part.

Of the three examples I have chosen, the key stage 4 group has the most complicated 'tech'. However, they have access to a cueing system which links all the technical aspects of the production, including the television monitor. Much time is spent getting this right and existing technical expertise within the group is much appreciated. They have also had help with the electrical effects from another member of staff (who, incidentally, has responsibility within the school for technology across the curriculum). The stage-manager and her sound and lighting operators have all performed these roles before but never on quite this scale. However, they know what is required of them and rehearse efficiently.

Performing — Telling the Story

All the groups have now made their plays. Everything is ready for the second part of the production process — the performance itself. As students step into the ritual space and begin, be it in the primary hall or the drama studio, they join a long tradition. The expectation of a school audience is an expectation shared by audiences as far apart as Indonesia and Broadway, the excitement of the players as they prepare to tell their story stirs Barong Play performers and West End actors every bit as much as it will motivate the groups in my three examples.

The idea of drama as story is most clearly evident in the Columbus play. The students have decided to tell the story of Columbus's famous landfall on Watling Island on 12 October 1492 from the islanders' point of view. The school audience, in this case four junior classes, become, in imagination, the next generation of islanders listening and watching the account of how the great wide birds came to the island and disgorged pale faced men with strange weapons, and how they took some of the islanders back into the bodies of the birds and sailed away with them.

Here, the use of a storyteller to link the scenes devised by the group makes the narrative structure very obvious. They have used other theatrical conventions, too. Speaking in English, they have decided to give Columbus and his crew a kind of gobbledygook to speak, a made-up language which helps to signify their strangeness and helps the audience to identify with the Indians' perception of events. The costumes of the Spanish

sailors are exaggerated, reconstructed from an islander perception with materials likely to have been available to them after
the ships' departure.

The text itself is made up of a mixture of scripted speech
and improvisation. With the help of the teacher, the students
have built a rhythmic beat into the narrator's lines (they looked
at sections of Longfellow's *Hiawatha* as part of their investigation) to give the narration a more formal quality. There are five
students speaking short sections of the narration, and they have
all learned their lines. The scenes of confrontation, in which all
the other students are involved, are improvized within an agreed
scenario, the students using their own natural modes of discourse in their attempts to understand the intruders' gobbledygook. There is much use of gesture for the group has learned
about the importance of non-verbal language. They use simple
percussion to punctuate events and to indicate a change of scene
or the passage of time.

The notated scenario with the sections of scripted narration
forms a secure structure for performance. The students are clear
at all times as to what they should do, and although the improvized scenes change and develop each time they are played, like
the actors in the *commedia*, the scenario ensures that the students
always know where a scene starts and where it must end. This
format gives scope for the creativity of the students — it is they
who have devised the piece — while providing, under the
guidance of the teacher, an effective dramatic framework within
which that creativity may be expressed.

That evening the lights go down on the invited audience
gathered for the *Motherland* performance. Parents and grandparents who disembarked in England from the West Indies in
the 1950s have come to hear their story told by a new generation. The lights go up on the central playing area, the music
plays out and the story begins. Thoughtful interpretation of the
original script backed up by meticulous rehearsing results in a
powerful presentation. Here, the script and its notated cueing
provide a more detailed framework than the Columbus scenario. However, there is no doubt that the performance has been
the students' own. Sensitive characterization has fleshed out the
thin traces of personality indicated by the written lines and the

direction by the teacher of some of the more difficult scenes has helped the students to appreciate the necessity of placing their ideas within a coherent and readable dramatic form. Next time, some of them will feel confident enough to take on this directorial role themselves.

At the end, the applause is both generous and sincere. Many in the audience have been deeply moved by the performance and the memories it has stirred. The students come together in the centre to take a bow and the house lights come up. Most of those present want to stay to discuss what they have seen and to share with the students their thoughts about the play. Many of the students are black; there is a deep rapport between them and the parents and grandparents who have been watching. The other students sense this, and realize, possibly for the first time, the significance of what they have achieved and the power of drama to move and evoke. No one in that studio will ever forget what was shared that evening.

A few weeks, later, the same studio space has been transformed with blocks and scaffolding into a constructivist labyrinth. Not one but three television monitors perch on the network of wires and poles, suspended in a spider's web of technology. No accident this. Investigation of theatre design (part of the project) revealed photographs and drawings of the sets of Meyerhold, and these celebrations of a machine age grabbed the imagination of the students tackling the theme of advertising. Here was just the visual metaphor they needed to express the age of technology. Wires and screens are substituted for the giant cogs and wheels of the Russian formalists in a highly abstract set which dominates one end of the studio. As the audience enter, lights flicker and the three screens play silent quiz shows. Over this, quietly, the sound-track of a fourth quiz show. Already, key performers in the group are at work at sound-mixers and lighting controls.

Suddenly, without warning, the lights go out. The screens display a succession of car commercials, a babble of Vauxhalls, Peugeots and Rovers. Rival voice-overs compete for our attention. Slowly a single spotlight comes up on an old woman standing alone at a bus-stop with her shopping. The piece has begun.

The students are successful in this sophisticated multi-media presentation. It is their good fortune that now, at the end of their secondary education, they have been able to draw upon a good primary drama experience (perhaps, six years ago, they were in the Columbus play) and a solid and coherent dramatic curriculum in the secondary school. Like their fellow students in visual art and music, they can see how their creative ability and understanding of dramatic art has developed over their time in school. They understand the potential of technology in drama and of those silent behind-the-scenes performers who can realize it, and they know that the craft of drama requires no less skill, knowledge and imagination than any other arts subject.

Each of my three examples has ended in a performance; I have tried to show how the production process works from the first idea to the completed text. However, as we shall see, performance is by no means the inevitable or necessary end result. The production process may be stopped or started at any point, its elements re-arranged to suit the teacher's pedagogic aim. Sometimes, or, more likely, probably, groups will not get much further than the editing stage. Education in drama, like education in any art form, is a slow process of experimentation, practice and rejection. The finished performance, like the concert or the exhibition or the dance evening is only one of many possible educational outcomes.

The Drama Laboratory

The idea of exploration is fundamental to arts education and drama is no exception. For this reason, in the drama lesson, the simple linear journey culminating in performance may be quite rare. After all, the drama teacher is unlikely to have a finished production in mind each time a group embarks on a theme. Instead, we may expect to find groups of students experimenting with ideas, trying them out to learn how they are received, returning to re-think and re-order their work in the light of early readings. Like a painter's preliminary sketches or a composer's first attempts at a score, although many, if not all, are rejected, each marks a stage in the creative development of the artists. Through this process of judgment and selection we learn how to manipulate the medium; we learn what works and what does not work.

The possibilities afforded by the model of drama–as–text for collaborative investigation and criticism as well as for the practical exploration of form and content lead me to suggest that we might regard the drama studio as a kind of experimental forum — a dramatic *laboratory*.

What would this laboratory be like? Unlike physics or chemistry, experiments in drama can take place at a high level with no specialized equipment apart from the human body. There has probably been no starker example of this than Jerzy Grotowski's influential Theatre Laboratory in Poland. Grotowski established the Theatre Laboratory in order to examine what he saw as the fundamental core of drama — 'what takes place between spectator and actor'.

It is no mere coincidence that our own theatre laboratory has developed from a theatre rich in resources — in which the plastic arts, lighting and music, were constantly exploited — into the ascetic theatre we have become in recent years: an ascetic theatre in which the actors and audience are all that is left.[15]

Using only the barest necessities in the way of costumes and props, Grotowski stretched his company of dedicated performers to the limits and in doing so managed to create dramas of astonishing power and originality. Without the pressure of production deadlines he was able to spend long periods in rehearsal and in the analysis of performance, finally abandoning the finished product altogether to concentrate exclusively on the experimental process from which it was derived.[16]

It is the principle behind all Grotowski's work — the examination of what takes place between spectator and actor — that I wish to propose as the basis for work in the drama laboratory.

In school, we will probably not wish to place quite such an emphasis on the ascetic as that advocated by Grotowski. Indeed, although we may want to spend time in the 'poor theatre', for it is on its bare stage that the mechanics of the audience/actor relationship are most clearly visible, we will also want to incorporate 'the plastic arts' in our dramatic experiments. Facilities to enable students to explore the importance of design and the possibilities afforded by lighting and sound should always be available. Any experiment requires a clear focus, so it is also important that there is a defined performance area, a space in the laboratory where audience and actors gather together to examine a text. This may be a circle marked on the floor or an area in front of a blank wall. The important thing is that it should be accepted as the place where experiments can be observed.

Although the stage-text is likely to be the form most frequently placed under the dramatic microscope, the centrality of television to students' experience of dramatic art suggests that there must also be ready access to the electronic-text. In practice, this will mean the provision of a video-cassette recorder (VCR) and a television monitor large enough for all to see.[17] Finally, because we shall also be examining the social-text, we shall need daylight in our laboratory.

In practice, the drama laboratory will not look very different from the average drama studio. Blackout is essential, although natural light should also be an option. Lighting may be only a few spotlights on stands or a simple ceiling rig; the important thing is that it should be safe, flexible and easy for students to use. Sound may be catered for with a portable cassette player so long as it has sufficient volume. The video monitor and VCR should be permanent fixtures backed up with a library of useful tapes, so that students become accustomed to electronic-texts as a source of instant reference.

The atmosphere and layout of the drama laboratory should stimulate a seriousness of purpose similar to that demanded by the science laboratory. Good drama, however spontaneous, requires a focus and discipline in its production no less rigorous than that required by a physics experiment. Comedy, as every successful comedian knows, is a serious business. We should also remember that the working space in which students learn how drama signifies meaning is itself a powerful signifier. The utmost care should be taken to ensure that what the students read from their environment is consistent with how we wish them to regard what they do within it.

No one who has worked in the theatre would suggest that making good dramas is easy. Long hours, punishing rehearsal schedules and meticulous attention to the text are the hallmarks of a successful production. At the same time, the rewards are surely self-evident. If students are to share in these rewards then they must understand that preparation and experiment in the drama classroom require similar periods of sustained concentration and effort. In one sense, all students, of whatever age, have ready access to drama; they can simply get up and do it. With commitment and hard work, however, students are also capable of high standards in drama. As teachers, we should be careful not to mistake 'getting up and doing it' for real achievement. In their production work we should encourage students to stretch their skills and creative capacities to the utmost so that they too may experience the rewards of real success.

Notes and References

1   Mayakovsky V. (1970) *How are Verses Made?* London, Jonathan Cape, p. 57. Quoted in: Wolf, J. (1981) *The Social Production of Art*, London, Macmillan, p. 13.

2   See Finlay-Johnson, H. (1911) *The Dramatic Method of Teaching*, London, Nisbet, p. 22. 'Having thus brought my school to a condition in which the inmates had really lost and forgotten the relationships of teacher and scholar, by substituting those of fellow-workers, friends and play-mates, I had now to set to work to use to full advantage this condition of affairs.' See also Slade, P. (1958) *An Introduction to Child Drama*, London, Hodder and Stoughton, p. 2. '[Drama] is a virile and exciting experience, in which the teacher's task is that of a loving ally.' For a clear and concise account of the 'teacher/facilitator', see O'Neill, C. and Lambert, A. (1982) *Drama Structures*, London, Hutchinson, pp. 21–22.

3   Slade, P. (1958) *op. cit.*, p. 39.

4   The philosopher R.G. Collingwood reminds us that craft

and art are not the same. For one thing, 'the craftsman knows what he wants to make before he makes it', (p. 16) whereas the artist may only discover what he or she wants to make in the process of making it. However, few artists would deny the importance of craft in the execution of their work. For a lucid exposition on this and other matters relating to the nature of arts, see Collingwood, R.G. (1958) *The Principles of Art*, Oxford, Oxford University Press.

5 In 1990, HMI noted that 'only a minority of primary schools have a well-developed policy and guidelines for their work in drama'. See Department of Education and Science (1990b) *Aspects of Primary Education: The Teaching and Learning of Drama*, London, HMSO.

6 For example, 'Drama is a process which does not aim to deliver a given body of knowledge but which is a way of exploring areas of learning and of life.' Morton, D. (1989) *Assessment in Drama*, City of Leeds Department of Education, p. 15.

7 I explore this problem more fully in Hornbrook, D. (1989) *Education and Dramatic Art*, Oxford, Basil Blackwell.

8 Interestingly, Andy Kempe proposes an alternative, although not dissimilar, model with three key elements — 'Making Plays', 'Putting on Plays' and 'Understanding Plays'. Kempe, A. (1990) *The GCSE Drama Handbook*, Oxford, Basil Blackwell, p. vi.

9 Many teacher assessment schemes for drama place much importance on group participation, and some I have seen in the secondary school grade very little else. The origins of the dilemma about what to evaluate in drama are traced in Hornbrook, D. (1989) *op. cit.* See also chapter 1, note 12.

10 Dodgson, E. (1984) *Motherland*, London, Heinemann. *Motherland* was originally devised by Elyse Dodgson and young people from the West Indian Women's Project at Vauxhall Manor School in South London. It was first performed at the Oval House in 1982. The *Motherland* project is a fine example of the production process in action within an educational context. 'Just as slave mothers handed down their experience of slavery to their daughters, so West

Indian mothers have handed down the experience of hardship and discrimination which they faced as early immigrants.... Many of those women were closely involved in the production throughout the rehearsal period. The multi-racial company met three times a week to read transcripts of the interviews and listen to the tapes. Through improvised drama we made the women's experiences our own. Excited by a particular aspect of the drama work girls would come back with new ideas, poems and songs sometimes scribbled on crumpled pieces of paper. These all became part of *Motherland*.'

11 As teachers know, reality tends to fall short of this paradigm. Despite educational drama's aspirations to the collective ideal, in most groups the assertive dominate and it is their creative intention that prevails. Arguments over casting may thus be settled on the basis of the group's internal hierarchy rather than any dramatic grounds.

12 While not specifically related to schools, Kenneth Rea's research into the training of directors exposes the ad hoc way in which people become directors. Chapter 4, 'How Directors Direct', is particularly revealing. See Rea, K. (1989) *A Better Direction*, London, Calouste Gulbenkian.

13 I am identifying here what in recent years has become common practice in European theatre. I am nevertheless aware that this is not the only model. We should remember that the history of the theatre reveals dramatists and actors taking responsibility for the creative direction of plays, as well as stage managers and prompters. The dominant role of the director as we now know it is usually taken to have its origins in the Duke of Saxe-Meiningen's company in the mid-nineteenth century. See Braun, E. (1982) *The Director and the Stage: From Naturalism to Grotowski*, London, Methuen.

14 For all its popularity, role-play will remain a servant of the curriculum rather than an element of it. As Stanislavski knew, requiring actors to speak 'off-the-cuff' as if they were the characters they intend to portray, is an invaluable aid to characterization. Re-named 'hot seating', this method

can serve the ends of many areas of the humanities curriculum. See National Curriculum Council (1990a) *English: Non-Statutory Guidance*, D12.

15 Grotowski, J. (1969) *Towards a Poor Theatre* (edited by Eugenio Barba), London, Methuen, pp. 32–33. In 1959, Jerzy Grotowski and the writer Ludwik Flaszen established the Theatre of Thirteen Rows in Opole, in southwest Poland. In 1965, the company moved to Wroclaw with the official status of 'Institute of Actor's Research', better known as the 'Theatre Laboratory'.

16 Grotowski's *Apocalypsis Cum Figuris* (1968) took several years to prepare. However, in Edward Braun's account of the production, we can see some indications as to how Grotowski's experimental approach might inform work in the drama laboratory. '... the actors responded to a network of interwoven myths, historical events, literary fable and everyday occurrences, which formed in their totality a multi-level parable of the human race. But without the actors who performed it, it would have ceased to exist — for on one level it was drawn uniquely from the life-experiences of the actors involved.... For most of the period of its creation there was no script as such: action was improvised, and speech as well where it was absolutely essential.' Braun, E. (1982) *op. cit.*, p. 197.

17 Teachers might like to add a camera to this list of TV electronics. My view is that the making of an electronic-text is a highly sophisticated operation requiring at the very least access to editing facilities. However, this is not to rule it out — excellent texts of this kind have been made in the classroom using minimal equipment — but simply to point again to the dangers of confusing one kind of text with another.

Chapter 5

The Dramatic Curriculum 2: Reception

A text is made of multiple writings, drawn from many cultures and entering into mutual relations of dialogue, parody, contestation, but there is one place where this multiplicity is focused and that is the reader ... A text's unity lies not in it origin but in its destination.

Roland Barthes, 1977[1]

Watching Plays

Once we have left school, few of us take part in plays. All of us, however, watch them incessantly. Most obviously, television offers us an almost continuous stream of dramatized fiction from the early morning until late at night. One result of this is that when they come to school young people already have a highly sophisticated understanding of the vocabulary of the electronic-text. They can read visual images and sound-tract with great speed and subtlety.[2] When the same young people are exposed to stage-texts, either in the theatre or in school when professional companies visit, unfamiliarity with a set of conventions which, although they may seem superficially similar, actually signify in radically different ways, means that the interpretative frameworks they have learned from film and television can often fail them. When it comes to their own production work, the tendency of students to revert to improvizations which simulate television forms — the domestic melodrama of the soap opera, for example — is an indication of their understandable desire to operate on familiar semiological ground.

The framework of production in drama outlined in the previous chapter is designed to help students become more proficient at the crafting of dramatic texts and in the telling of their stories. We now need to explore ways in which students may also develop as readers of drama, as audiences to other people's stories. Because we are dealing here predominantly with the production and reception of stage-texts, I shall propose ways in which students already comfortable with the electronic-text may also learn to read live dramas — how they might become *stage literate*.

Perhaps the first thing to acknowledge is the complexity of the stage-text. So long as the play remains in the form of a script, its material existence is confined to words on the page. As in the novel and the poem, these words are the signifiers of meaning, allowing us to enter in our imaginations the world delineated for us by the playwright. However, this world is sketched lightly, dialogue and stage directions the only guides in our interpretative journey. The play in the book is merely a map of an infinite number of potential realizations.

Transcribed into a living text on the stage, however, the play presents us with a multitude of signifiers, of which the written word (if it appears at all) will only be one. A printed sentence in the script transforms into an ephemeral utterance, spoken in a particular way by a particular actor at a particular place within a particular setting at a particular moment. As the line hangs in the air, we are its witnesses. We read it within its stage context, unconsciously interpreting its sound against a background of countless other signifiers. The mood evoked by the lighting or the music, the attitude of the actor towards the character, the colour of her coat; all these we take into account as we engage in the process of making sense of what is enacted before us.

The more we understand the conventions of a stage-text the more deeply we can engage with it. As a student, I once attended a Noh Theatre performance. Once my fascination with the exotic display had worn off, and as I had no idea how to interpret its conventions, I am ashamed to admit I became rather bored. Our students can be similarly alienated by unfamiliar forms. If we wish to help them to become stage literate then we must make sure not only that they encounter as wide a range of stage-texts as possible but also that they are suitably prepared for these encounters.

In order to stimulate the development of stage literacy we must find a way of systematically approaching stage perform-ances. As it is, students in their English lessons are frequently encouraged to respond to performance rather as if it were little more than animated literature. At secondary level, this academic approach addresses questions such as 'How successfully was the character of Desdemona portrayed?', and tends to ignore factors which do not relate to the study of a play as words on the page. Alternatively, students of drama are often simply asked to ex-press their feelings about a performance. However, our engage-ment with drama involves far more than watching notated characters come to life, and although we do, of course, make a subjective response to what we see and hear, that response rests on a culturally shared agreement about the meaning of signs.[3] If we are outside that agreement, as I was at my first experience of Japanese theatre, our engagement will be an impoverished one.

Everything we see or hear we subject to interpretation. We measure up an experience against others we have had or heard about in order to try to make sense of what is happening. Every day we read the complex language of human gesture and utter-ance and interpret it in the context in which it is performed. As the lead player in a familiar social-text, the new teacher stepping out before a particular classroom audience for the first time will be assessed and categorized by watchers and listeners eager to make sense out of what they perceive. Every word spoken, every action, will be read carefully before being placed within a developing framework of meaning against which all the teacher's subsequent acts will be interpreted.

Some of the pleasure we have from watching plays comes from drama's capacity to show us others engaging in these interpretative encounters. Much dramatic comedy, for instance, derives its humour from *mis*interpretation. Examples can be

found from Shakespeare's 'disguise' comedies, where the characters 'read' a woman as if she were a man, to contemporary
television series, such as *Fawlty Towers*, where Basil Fawlty's
mis-reading of situations guarantees his discomfort and our
entertainment.

Most electronic and stage-texts depend upon their audience's experience of everyday social encounters. At the same
time, both have their own sets of conventions which we read
simultaneously with the signifiers reproduced from social-texts.
When we watch a film we read the social signifiers (a character's
expression, inappropriate behaviour) alongside the signifiers of
the medium itself (the close-up, the music on the sound-track)
so that unconsciously both become fused into the meaning we
make of what we experience. The same is true of the stage-text.
Not only do we assess what the characters say and do against
what we know of life, but we also read the relative placing of
the actors, the shape and colour of the set, the music, the level
of lighting and the pacing of the scene as part of our overall
interpretation of the play. In principle, this is as true of the class
play as it is of the professional theatre production. According to
Jonathan Miller,

> ... we are participating in a representational system, and
> we are reading the play systematically as something that
> stands for what we suppose it to be. In order to do this
> we have to recognise the existence of a *frame* within
> which what is to be seen is taken as representational and
> beyond which everything to be seen is regarded as part of
> the real world.[4]

The frame makes anything within it *significant*.[5] It may be
a ritual circle, a trestle stage, or, as in many forms of street
theatre, simply what is indicated by the performers themselves
as they move about amongst the crowd. When we are in the
presence of a proscenium arch we may be reasonably assured
that it will mark the boundaries of the imagined world of the
play. Even here, directors will sometimes deliberately challenge
this convention, by having actors entering through the audience,

for example. Peter Brook's famous 1968 production of Seneca's *Oedipus* at the Old Vic had the chorus spread out around the auditorium. Although strategies of this kind deliberately break the rules, however, they are usually well signified; after an initial surprise we are able to incorporate them into our overall reading. As I have already indicated, in the hurly-burly of the drama lesson this important principle of framing is sometimes forgotten.

As well as a spatial frame, the story must be contained within a temporal frame. We must know when it begins and when it ends. Again, in traditional European theatre curtains rise and fall, lights go up and down, prologues and epilogues announce the arrival and departure of the actors. Other theatre forms employ dances, trumpet calls or simple exhortation to gain the attention of an audience. After the bows, the passing around of the hat may well be the unambiguous indication that the performance has come to an end.

A Framework for Audience Response

By looking into one of these frames and separating out the performance into its constituent elements we should be able to see more clearly what is involved in the reception of a drama by an audience. Then, by taking each of these elements of performance in turn and examining the audience's relationship with it, a clearer understanding of how the stage-text does its work and achieves its effect should emerge.

The framework for audience response outlined in this chapter and introduced in figure 5, is a set of guidelines for responding to plays of all kinds designed to be broad enough to encompass the simplest and the most elaborate performance. While no conceptual distinction is made between the classroom improvization prepared for an audience and the professional production, as the complexity of students' response will vary depending on their age and their experience, teachers may wish to modify the framework to suit a particular group. I have tried here to keep things simple by opting for a small number of categories which

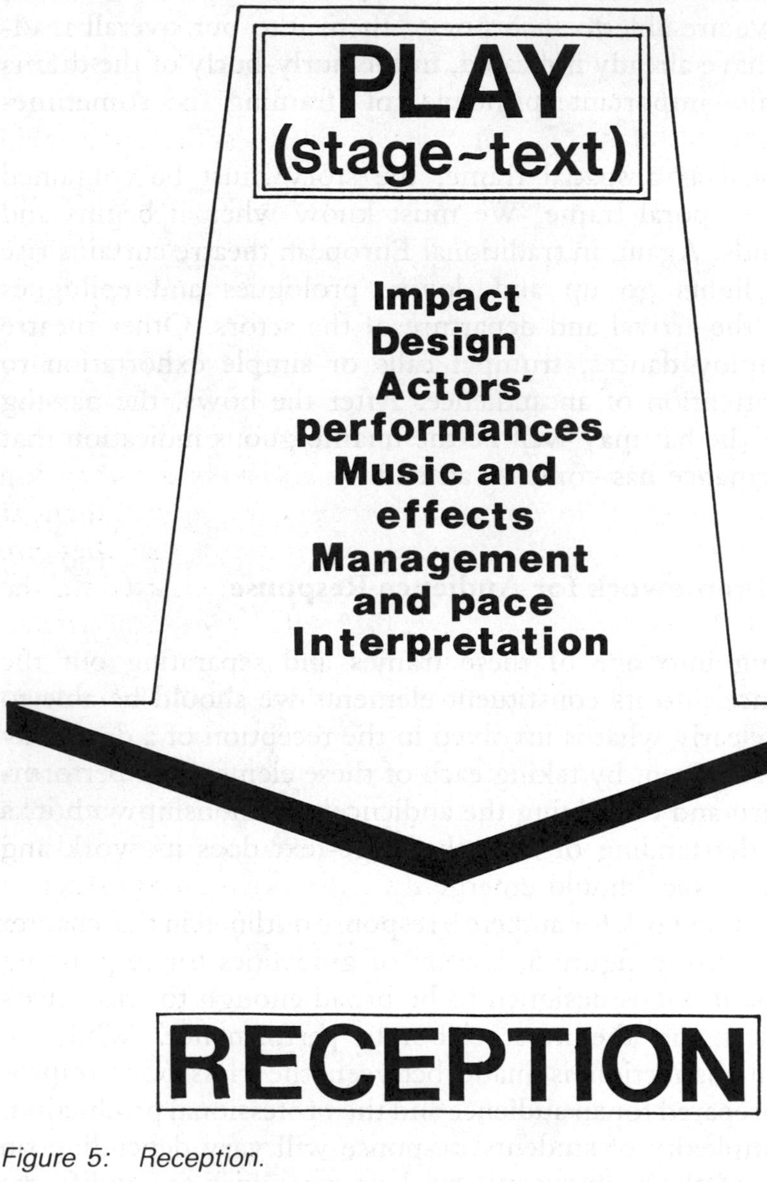

PLAY
(stage~text)

Impact
Design
Actors'
performances
Music and
effects
Management
and pace
Interpretation

RECEPTION

Figure 5:   Reception.

are then elaborated and developed with some examples and sign-post questions for students which can be selected and adapted as required.[6]

After recording a first response, students should set about addressing specific questions relating to the performance. As indicated, these should include discussion of such key signifiers as the setting, the acting, the effects and the general management of the performance. The answers to these questions will contribute to an overall critical interpretation.

Impact — What Was My Initial Response to the Play?

It is important that by analyzing a performance we do not bury the feelings initially evoked by it. The delight expressed by young children watching a class play is a precious thing. Although teachers of dramatic art will want students to develop their powers of dramatic perception, they will not wish them at the same time to become so bound by semiotics that they are unable any more to express spontaneous pleasure. After all, the point of learning how plays achieve their effect is to stimulate an interest in drama and not to smother it.

Depending on their age, students should initially be encouraged to respond to a performance as freely as possible. A painting or a poem might be a suitable form of response, or even a drama. For older students, jottings in their drama notebooks might be appropriate. At this stage, discussion and essay writing should be avoided. This is the only time when an unmediated response can be recorded and students should be at liberty to express their feelings in whatever way they choose.

Signpost questions:

> What did you expect?
> How did you react?
> How did the rest of the audience react?
> What were the best moments?
> What were the most boring parts?
> What images have you retained?

Design — What Did the Play Look Like?

A visit to the theatre or to a performance by a touring company in school will often leave students with vivid images of the set and costumes. The more spectacular the production, the more these perceptions will be likely to dominate their overall impressions. Like Victorian audiences who marvelled at the on-stage train crash or real horse racing, a dazzling visual assault can sometimes distract us from weaknesses elsewhere. In the classroom, on the other hand, the reverse will often be true. Students' work may well be presented against a truly unmemorable background of torn black-out curtains and broken furniture. While in the former case the setting may distract us from an appreciation of the play itself, in the latter the background simply disappears from the consciousness of the audience.

There is much to be learned from both extremes. The first principle is that design must always be the servant and not the master of a production. According to Brecht, the good designer 'knows better than anyone that whatever does not further the narrative harms it'.[7] The questions that should be directed at the design as a whole, as well as to individual aspects of it, should start from this premise. Brecht is surely right to direct our attention away from design as the crafting of spectacle or illusion — Beerbohm Tree's ostentatiously upholstered *A Midsummer Night's Dream* with real rabbits a famous example — and towards the idea of the designer as 'an ingenious story-teller'. The set, the costumes and the stage properties are all signifiers in the story being told by the actors and should collude with it rather than act as a diversion, however well-contrived. There is much wisdom in Michael Green's ironic description of the amateur lighting designer who 'is not concerned with lighting either the actors or the set, but with lighting the lights, so that people will say, "What wonderful lighting"'.[8]

The contrast with the classroom could hardly be more marked. Here time and resources invariably dictate a minimalist approach. It is probably fair to say that for most classroom plays, improvised or otherwise, design considerations do not figure highly. Students are happy to accept an unspoken convention which allows a dramatic reality to be established out of the most unpromising surroundings. Like the Madagascan Hira Gasy performers or the English Mummers, students make their dramas amidst the familiar clutter of everyday life.

How things look, however, is as significant in the drama studio as it is on the professional stage. That students do not wear costume, that the set is no more than a few classroom chairs and that the properties are mostly mimed, suggests a quite distinct set of conventions which are no less conventions for being unconscious. This is most apparent when for some reason an improvization is transferred out of context. Placed in a well-lit theatre (as part of a drama festival, for example), what seemed acceptable enough in the classroom suddenly becomes difficult to read. The bowls, the knives and forks, adequately mimed back at school, now seem a puzzling absence. In the theatre, the classroom furniture which happily signified a domestic suite in the drama studio, now suggests, well, a class-room. The students' fashionable clothes are impossible to read coherently in the context of the middle-aged family they are trying to represent. Here, too, however unwittingly, the design is working against the narrative.

It is most important that students understand how design influences the meaning of a text. Simple rules of positioning (such as the dominating effect of the upstage centre position on the proscenium stage), the need for consistency in the use of convention (a walking stick mimed by a character in one scene cannot arbitrarily be replaced by a real one in another without sending out confusing messages), the use of costume signifiers like hats to establish characters, are all examples of basic design considerations. With older students, teachers will wish to con-sider wider aesthetic factors, such as the employment of colour, shape and lighting.

Above all, students should learn to read the signs embodied in the design of the stage text as naturally as they read those contained in the dialogue and gestures of the actors.

Signpost questions:

Where does the performance take place?
What is the relationship between the performance space and
    the audience space?

How is 'off-stage' indicated?

How does the design help to indicate the play's imagined location(s)?

What are the aesthetic principles (colour, shape, etc.) informing the design?

How does the lighting contribute to the narrative?

What are the conventions governing the use of costumes and properties?

Actors' Performance — How Do They Tell the Story?

When we come to read a stage-text, the performance of the actors will be a primary signifier. Also, although we may be concerned to foster in our students a commitment to collective as opposed to solo achievement, the fact remains that powerful individual performances do impress us when we see them, as in this nineteenth-century example.

> It must be unanimously granted that Mr. Henry Irving's performance is most striking.... The gradual stupefaction, the fixed eye, the head bent down on the chest, and the crouching humility before a stronger will in the one scene; and the ugly picture of a dead man's face, convulsed after a dream, in which he thought he was hanged, are touches of genuine art.... The other characters are comparatively subordinate ...[9]

It is tempting to ask what Irving would have scored in a school drama practical examination — not very highly for group work, I imagine!

What we should learn from this is that when considering actors' contribution to a text, we must pay attention both to the collective and the individual. As with design, the actors serve the narrative; we must be careful not to allow the hypnotic effect of a charismatic performance like Irving's to cloud this principle, in school or out of it. At the same time, the story is not well served by actors who cannot communicate it to us, or who, through insufficient mastery of their craft, transmit contradictory messages. The actor who wishes still to appear glamorous while playing a victim of homelessness or who expresses anger in her voice but not in her posture, are simple examples of this kind of semiological confusion.

I think it is fair to say that the minimum expectation we would have of a student violinist playing in a trio would be an ability to play the notes as they are indicated in tune and with reasonable accuracy, to come in on time, and to fulfil the violin's part in the overall balance of the piece. The appreciable absence of any one of these conditions would be likely to make the total performance very difficult to read. In drama, the actor has to demonstrate skills of a similar kind. Accurate and clear vocal and physical communication (voice, gesture, timing), careful attention to the directions agreed during the production process and the integration of character into the overall narrative theme are all prerequisites of a coherent dramatic performance. Once again, weakness in any one may destabilize the semiological balance of the text and lead to an overall communication failure.

These conditions apply equally to the drama classroom and the theatre. Let us return for a moment to our primary group and their Columbus piece. One student, let us call him Mark, has a small part to play as one of the Indian villagers. To help the story, it has been arranged in rehearsal that as the Indians confront Columbus's party, his character becomes frightened and at a crucial moment jumps forward to attack the visitors. He is restrained by his companions.

Mark's intervention at that point, although only a tiny part of the whole, helps to signify the tension between the two groups. To achieve this goal, he must first convey to us that he is sufficiently frightened to make such a spontaneous attack. As an audience, we must be able to read this fear in his posture and his voice, or his action may seem puzzlingly unmotivated. We may, for instance, think he is a madman, given to irrational outbursts. Second, he must remember to make his move at the correct moment, or he will throw the response of the other actors. The coordination of Mark's outburst and the defensive movements of the sailors is essential if we are to read tension into the incident. Finally, Mark's character, however sketchily drawn, must identify him with the Indians. We will read him from the moment he appears with the others. Inconsistencies (such as smiling at a friend who is playing a Spaniard) will draw inappropriate attention to him and divert us from the narrative.

I hope it is clear by this example that I am not suggesting that every student performer must attend a course at drama school. None of the simple disciplines indicated here is beyond the average primary child. The point I wish to emphasize, however, is that students should learn to judge an actor's performance in terms of his or her contribution to the overall narrative. Good acting cannot stand apart from the story that is being told.

Signpost questions:

What was the style of the acting? (e.g. naturalistic, like a circus, mime, etc.)
How did the actors indicate what their characters were like?
Could you hear and understand what they said?
How were the characters' relationships with each other indicated by the actors?
How successful were the actors in telling you the story?
Did you notice any special techniques used by the actors?

Music and Effects — How Do They Enhance the Story?

It has been said that music and stage effects are most effective when they are so integrated within the narrative that we fail to notice them. To some extent this is true, as we know from film and television. The subtle introduction of music onto the soundtrack at a strategic point in the story can stimulate our emotional involvement, and many clever effects (such as the candle concealing an electric light revealed in Truffaut's *Day for Night*) pass unnoticed. Some playwrights indicate the use of music, as in the last act of Chekhov's *Three Sisters*, and others make complicated technical demands on the production team, like the collapsing furniture in Brecht's *The Wedding* or the legs which fill the stage in Ionesco's *Amédée, or How to Get Rid of It*.

In school, recorded music is sometimes used to accompany

dramatic performances and BBC sound-effects records can often be found tucked away in corner of the drama cupboard. Similarly, vocal sound and simple percussion are all perfectly accessible to teachers at both primary and secondary levels. Students should be sensitive to the way musical and other effects are deployed and learn to discriminate between those which contribute to the narrative and those which simply draw attention to themselves.

Signpost questions:

How was music used in the play? Was it live or recorded?
How did the music contribute to the story or to the mood of a scene?
What special effects did you notice?
Were the effects used, successful?

Management and Pace — How is the Story Controlled?

When we consider the management of a production we are looking at all those organizational aspects which hold it together. At a most basic level, as an audience, we must know where to sit or stand and where to look and when to leave. The actors must know where and when to come on and to whom they are telling their story. All these matters will be relatively unproblematic in a conventional theatre, where agreement and custom will normally ensure a correlation between the respective expectations of audience and performers. However, school productions, particularly those of a more informal kind, will sometimes reveal that insufficient attention has been paid to such fundamentals. A whole class arriving noisily after the performance has started, lack of chairs so that some students find themselves sitting in the performance space, rapturous concluding applause when there is still a scene to play, and so on; all such distractions hinder the essential communication between actors and audience.

As well as these front-of-house considerations, on-stage events require a careful hand. Long and noisy scene changes, ill-timed lighting and sound cues, late entrances, are all signs of inadequate stage-management, and while they are often the source of much subsequent merriment, they too can interfere drastically with the transmission of the text.

The pace of the production itself is largely the responsibility of the director and the actors (although weak stage-management will not help). Unimaginative, pedantic directing can slow the text down so that those vital elements of a good story — tension, expectation and intrigue — cease to engage us. The director has a particular task to move the text towards or away from climax and productions are sometimes marred by a failure to attend sufficiently to this important responsibility. Similarly, actors who pause too long, respond carelessly to cues, or give languid or otherwise indulgent performances, can quickly lose an audience's attention.

Pace is not the same as speed. I once suffered a very tired performance of *Les Miserables* which nevertheless went like an express train (probably driven by the actor's desire to get to the pub). Good pace suggests the presence of acute attention and commitment on the part of the cast within the context of tight, intelligent direction.

Signpost questions:

Did the show start on time?
What parts of the performance most/least captured your attention? Why?
Were the technical cues on time?
Did the front-of-house management go smoothly?

Interpretation — What Sense Do We Make of the Play?

At all ages, students should be made aware that any performance is the result of choices; that scenes can be played different-ly, cast with other actors, set in another style or period. The ability to contextualize a performance within a growing drama-tic vocabulary and at the same time to imagine how it might have been different is the basis of successful interpretation.

In drama, the word 'interpretation' is often used to describe the way a particular theme or script has been realized in production. The stage-text itself may well be an 'interpretation' of this kind. Actors interpret parts; directors interpret scripts. However, when we watch a play, we too interpret. In our minds, we translate the complex semiology of what we see and hear into something meaningful. Furthermore, any subsequent account we give of our experience at the play will itself be the subject of interpretation by others. All these different levels of interpretation should be taken into consideration in this final element of the framework for audience response.

Whereas our initial response to a performance may be highly idiosyncratic and subjective (I may simply dislike one of the actors or have an uncomfortable seat) our interpretation of any particular stage-text is likely to be more considered. As we watch, all kinds of related experiences may be brought to bear: our knowledge of the script, our memories of other productions, reviews we have read, what we have been taught about the play or read in the programme notes, our expectations of a particular playwright, director or actor. Subsequently, we are likely to discuss the performance with others and listen to alternative views. We may re-read the critics or ask our teacher what he or she thought.

The result of this complex cross-referencing is that our interpretation will be less subjective than *inter*-subjective, still uniquely ours, but measured out within the framework of implicit cultural agreement about what things mean; as we saw in chapter 2, the meaning of dramatic signifiers is essentially shared.[10] I reiterate this here because it is sometimes said that response to drama (or any art) is *solely* a matter of individual taste ('personal meaning'). Instead, I would argue (*pace* Wittgenstein) that when we express views about a drama, the language we speak and conventions we use themselves bind us to a community of meaning which is a pre-condition of intelligibility. Thus, while liking or disliking a play is surely a personal matter, it is quite legitimate to suggest that a student's interpretation might be perhaps ill-judged or even simply mistaken. What is often forgotten is the role that any teacher plays in the process of acculturation. Like production, reception is learned.

Students should understand, therefore, that it is possible both to express a spontaneous reaction to a performance and to offer a considered interpretation. A student who describes a show as 'rubbish' is likely to be expressing personal dislike rather than considered judgment. Pressed, he may turn out to have quite liked the costumes, admired one of the performances and thought the music was 'great'. It is this initial discrimination between aspects of the production that is the starting point of interpretation.

The signpost questions already listed in this chapter may then form the basis of more detailed thoughts about the play. As students progress through the dramatic curriculum, they should be able to address these questions within an increasingly wide frame of dramatic reference which will inform their interpretation. Young children, for example, will have no difficulty distinguishing between clowning and the more serious parts of a play, while older students should be able to identify genre and consider, if appropriate, the relationship between the stage-text and its notation. Once again, students will only acquire the necessary vocabulary to accomplish these forms of interpretation if they are offered a dramatic curriculum which exposes them to a comprehensive range of culturally and historically diverse dramatic forms. They will develop their dramatic imaginations if they are encouraged to allow their experience as spectators to enrich their own creative production work.

The means whereby students' interpretations can be expressed are extremely varied. It should not be assumed that the traditional 'lit crit' essay (still favoured by many examination boards) is the only appropriate form of response. Mostly, discussion and debate will be more than adequate. Once again, students might be encouraged to interpret their experience through other art forms: drawing or painting, for example, or poetry or even music. Neither is there any reason why drama itself should not be a suitable vehicle for such an interpretation.

Interpretation will inevitably entail judgment. By saying what we made of an experience in the theatre we imply a view. The important thing is that students should learn how to exercise this judgment carefully, taking account of all the factors which contribute to the appreciation of a text.

Signpost questions:

To what extent has your initial response been modified?
On reflection, what did the play most make you think about?
Was the performance an interpretation? If so, how successful was it?
If you had been the director, what would you have done differently?
What are the differences between your interpretation of what you saw and others you have read or heard?
What have you learned about drama from the production?
In what medium would you most like to express your thoughts and feelings about the play?

The Context of Learning

My proposals for dramatic art acknowledge and relate to the four categories outlined in the first volume of this series, *Living Powers* — making, presenting, responding and evaluating — as well as the two fundamental aspects of arts education — making and appraising — identified by the National Curriculum Council Arts in Schools Project (see appendix 1).[11] The significance of this is that drama teachers adopting the framework for dramatic art should not find the establishment of curricular links with the other arts — particularly the performing arts — problematic. Music teachers have become accustomed to a music curriculum based upon composing, performing and listening, while dance teachers are mostly happy with their model of choreographing, performing and viewing.[12] The framework for dramatic art sits easily alongside all of these.

This correspondence should help teachers who believe that students should continue to have the opportunity to participate in a balanced arts curriculum, whatever the exigencies of the national curriculum. At primary level, drama will remain an invaluable focus for practical activities involving all the arts, while for secondary drama specialists, being able to share a vocabulary with colleagues in music, visual art and dance is a prerequisite of a successful arts faculty.

We have already seen how production in drama can incorporate many different art forms and how, when we watch a play, the design and the music may well be highly important signifiers. Education in drama should encourage students to develop a broad aesthetic knowledge and an awareness of how all the arts can contribute to a dramatic text. Many dance forms, for example, have a strong dramatic component. Classical Indian dance has a comprehensive mimetic language and, for some students, may be a way into non-verbal theatre and of realizing the potential of their bodies as expressive instruments. Music, too, can add an extra dimension to production work; students of all ages should be made aware of the power of music to enrich dramatic action and to move an audience. (Also, the skills of the musician, like those of the dancer, serve as a reminder of the importance of practice and application.) Similarly, students need to learn how design affects the essential relationship between performers and their environment. In drama, as in visual art, shape, colour and texture are key communicators of mood and ideas. All this, together with an understanding of drama's place in a wider culture, amounts to a *contextualizing* of experience which is an essential and embracing aspect of the dramatic curriculum.

For all it might be said to be the most comprehensive and inclusive of all art forms, drama (in education) has tended in the past to play down the contextual element and has kept the other arts somewhat at arm's length. Instead, drama's historical allegiances in schools have meant that drama teachers have often concentrated on the aims they have traditionally shared with colleagues in English — language development, imaginative empathy, ethical and social development, and so on. As we have seen, while this has led to the emergence of many useful teaching methodologies, it has diverted the energies of drama teachers away from the wider arts community.[13]

For these reasons, the curriculum outlined in this book may unsettle some teachers who are comfortable with the use of drama for the development of social skills and the exploration of issues. Despite reassurances that my proposed dramatic curriculum is based upon a theory of art which sets out to bring together the aesthetic and the material, they may still be concerned that the re-orientation of drama as an arts subject with its own distinctive skills, knowledge and practices will mean its emasculation as an agency for social and moral learning.

No subject or set of practices can claim that engagement with it will *necessarily* bring about a change of attitude or perception. Even the most fertile curriculum fields can, in some hands, become pedagogic deserts rather than the oases of enlightenment intended by their proponents. We should remember that dramatic role-play, however earnest in execution, can just as easily be dull and superficial as stimulating and provocative.

Good teachers will use whatever resources they can command to capture and sustain the interest of their students. They will do this in geography, in French, in religious education, in maths. *Any* subject may stimulate learning about pertinent issues. It is just that the arts, those profound articulations of collective sensibility, can sometimes lead us into otherwise inaccessible recesses and illuminate the paradoxes of the human condition with the starting clarity of recognition identified in chapter 2.

Dramatic art is supreme in this; plays, after all, are *about* something. As the good English teacher will want to achieve a balance between the questions raised by poetry and the means poets employ to achieve their effect, so the good drama teacher will not wish to submerge the themes and issues of a play in a discussion about the lighting. Both will choose material that is intelligent and thoughtful, poems and plays that they consider intrinsically worth attention. Both will understand that form and content in the arts are inextricably linked.

It could be said that the content of a poem or a play should always determine its form — that form is then the means whereby we gain access to content. In this respect, many drama teachers would probably agree with the Marxist poet and critic Ernst Fischer who argues that a preoccupation with artistic form will never get us to the roots of art 'unless it recognises that content — that is to say, in the last instance, the social element — is the decisive style-forming factor in art'.[14]

This is not to say that a certain form is 'latent' in any given content, as some drama-in-education theorists have suggested. All form is interpretation and no one form is necessarily right for any given content. The Holocaust, for example, may be equally well interpreted through the harrowing naturalism of Martin Sherman's *Bent*, in the tuneful camaraderie of Joshua Sobol's *Ghetto* or in the horrific evidence so cooly laid before us in Peter Weiss's *The Investigation*.

Similarly, although there is no 'right' way of directing Shakespeare, or any other playwright, a production which obscures or distorts the issues of a play may be rightly classed a failure. Of course, in reality there is a very narrow boundary between distortion and revelation. A production I once saw of David Hare's *Fanshen* which eschewed the simple directness indicated in the script for Oriental make-up and Chinese accents seemed to me to have quite fundamentally missed the point. On the other hand, Peter Brook's extraordinary 1970 *Midsummer Night's Dream* at Stratford in which 'the tittuping fairies and fat jolly avuncular actors wearing asses' heads [were] flushed smartly into the Avon like so much effluent[15] brought a refreshing clarity to a play for too long buried beneath acres of painted undergrowth and Mendelssohn.

It is in the process of interpretation that the wider learning associated with dramatic art takes place. The questions that face students as they attempt to match form to ideas in the production process extend naturally to the judgments they make as an audience about the interpretative decisions of others; the one process informs the other. Successful engagement in production or reception requires of students both an acute awareness of the issues involved and an understanding of the variety of dramatic forms within which they may be expressed. If drama teachers choose their source material well, then education in drama can be as broad and as enlightening as the field of drama itself.

By way of illustration, I should like to conclude this chapter with two stories.

A primary class was going to see a production of Tony Harrison's *The Nativity* mounted by a local secondary school.[16] In preparation for the visit, the teacher had first introduced her 10-year-olds to the Bible stories that make up the play. Much of this turned out to be question and answer — many of her class had some knowledge of the stories already. The teacher then divided her class into five groups each of which she gave a name — Grocers, Millers, Shipwrights, Tailors, Goldsmiths.

The teacher explained briefly how from medieval times, tradesmen and craftsmen had formed professional associations called guilds to maintain standards and protect their interests. After some general discussion (which ranged over the absence of women from the guilds, masters and apprentices, the difference between salaried professionals and weekly wage-earners, what a guild of teachers might be like, and what the Guildhall was for) the teacher asked each group to go away and decide how standards and interests in their particular 'guild' were to be guaranteed. These ideas had to be written down as a formal code of conduct and also represented pictorially in the form of a painted banner. A representative from each group then came forward with the banner to announce the code of the 'guild', beginning with the words, 'We, Members of the Honourable Company of (here they named their group) do declare the following code of conduct ...'

With the students now firmly identified with a 'guild', the teacher described how medieval guilds each took on responsibility for a play in the annual Mystery Cycle. She then allocated one bible story to each group — The Creation to the Grocers, Cain and Abel to the Millers, Noah to the Shipwrights, The Shepherds' Pageant to the Tailors and Herod the Great to the Goldsmiths. She told the class that the performances of the plays would reflect medieval custom and be confined to the rostrum she had set up in the hall and its immediate vicinity. The only scenery would be what the 'guilds' could make, and the teacher asked the students to notate their work in the form of a scenario for each play. With all this in mind, the class set about working out how to tell the stories.

This class was familiar with drama so the students had already acquired the elements of a dramatic vocabulary. Some decided to employ a narrator, others used masks. Each play offered its own challenge. For example, how do you show the creation of the universe with six 10-year-olds on a rostrum in the corner of the hall? However, with the help of the teacher (who was not afraid to intervene when advice was needed) all rose to the occasion.

When the plays were ready, two neighbouring classes were invited in to watch. By now, there were two rostra, one at each end of the hall, so that the performance could be continuous. The plays happened alternately, one group quietly setting-up while another performed. The standing, or 'promenade', audience simply moved to the appropriate stage. The costumes were taken from the dressing-up box or improvised, the scenery minimal. On an easel beside each performance was proudly pinned the 'guild' banner.

The cycle of five Mystery Plays was a great success and repeat performances were demanded for parents and other students in the school. The five scenarios were written up carefully and preserved in a book.

On the day following their final performance the students went to *The Nativity*. As with any outside visit, they had been immensely looking forward to it. Some wore the badges of their 'guilds'. With their own experience as makers and performers and their knowledge of the Mystery Plays, the teacher knew that they would make a more than usually discerning audience.

The production was excellent. There was a good sized audience in the hall which moved about the space as the story unfolded. The director had kept faith with the simplicity of the National Theatre's production, and the cast wore the working clothes of ordinary people. There was dancing and a lively folk band.

Going back on the coach, the teacher was assiduous in expressing no view of the production, despite heavy pressure from others with no such reservations! She knew that letting the play make its own impact and allowing time for unstructured response was an important first stage in the appreciation process.

Next day began with an open discussion about what they had seen. They thought Herod was horrid and had laughed at the shepherds. Inevitably, comparisons were made. To get the best out of the talk, the teacher wrote up 'design', 'actors' performances', 'music and effects' 'management and pace' and 'interpretation' as headings, and insisted on dealing with each in turn. Helped by their extensive preparation, the students' comments were often very perceptive. One boy thought that having live music made all the difference as it helped the audience to feel involved. A girl thought the lighting focused attention, even though, as she pointed out, they would not have had it in the Middle Ages.

After a while, the teacher began to direct the conversation towards some new avenues she wanted to explore. She asked about the language. Could they understand it? Not all of it, was the general consensus, but 'as we knew the stories, it didn't really matter.' They were not sure why it was in verse. Taking up the script, the teacher read some of Herod's lines which she had also written up for the class to see:

The prince of the planets that proudly is pight
Shall brace forth his beams that our shelter shall know;
The moon at my might, he musters his might;
And kaisers in castles great kindness me show.[17]

Speaking a line in turn, and with the help of a strong beat, the students quickly got the idea of the rhythm and of the use of alliteration. So excited were they by this, admittedly rather noisy, discovery that they failed to notice that the teacher had covered up the lines. Without realizing, they had learned them. 'So *that's* why they wrote in verse.'

Finally, the teacher asked the students to return to the scenarios of their own plays and to attempt to flesh them out with similar strong, rhythmic, and, if they could manage it, alliterative, verse for the characters to speak.

The story is not over, although I shall end my telling of it there. Let me just say that the students came up with fine Miracle Plays which they wanted to perform again at Christmas, this time in their fully-scripted versions. From the project came work in history, English and religious education — the morality of a God who instructs a father to sacrifice his son became a real issue — as well as a great deal of learning in drama.

My second story concerns a visit by a group of 16-year-olds

from an inner-city comprehensive school to a performance of Timberlake Wertenbaker's *Our Country's Good*.[18] This story begins with the teacher reading some lines from the play to the assembled class. A lone Aboriginal Australian describes the arrival of the First Convict Fleet in Botany Bay in 1788.

> A giant canoe drifts onto the sea, clouds billowing from upright oars. This is a dream which has lost its way. Best to leave it alone.[19]

For a moment after the teacher has stopped reading, the students in the drama studio stand motionless and in silence, trying, perhaps, to imagine what the first sighting of that little convoy would have been like. Nothing more is said. The students file out quietly and board the coach for the theatre.

The drama teacher had decided to give her drama option group only the briefest of introductions to the play. The previous week a colleague from the History Department had come to talk about the discovery of Australia and the subsequent transportation of convicts (while she had done some drama with his history class) and later she had handed round some rather dusty copies of *The Recruiting Officer* she had found in the English Department. She had asked the students to read Farquhar's play at home, believing that few, if any, would do so. On the afternoon of the theatre visit she quizzed them mildly about *The Recruiting Officer* and was surprised that a substantial number seemed at least to know the story and the names of the major characters. That was enough. As it figured so prominently in what they would be seeing, the teacher realized that her students would be disadvantaged by not knowing *something* about Farquhar's play; at the same time she did not want them to lose their empathy with the convicts by being too many steps ahead of them.

Just before they left, she had read her group the short speech quoted above, reminding the students not to forget that the Aboriginal people had lived peacefully in Australia for thousands of years before the arrival of Captain Cook. 'Listen for their voice in the play, too,' she said.

It was three days before she saw the group again. They were anxious to talk about the performance, but before letting them do so the teacher reminded them of the Aboriginal voice and gave out copies of the four short Aboriginal speeches in the play. 'What does the Aborigine mean when he says in the last speech — "Perhaps we have been wrong all this time and this is not a dream after all."?' Many students had been so absorbed in the main action of the play that they had forgotten the references to the smallpox epidemic which was killing the native inhabitants. One or two knew a little about Aboriginal dream culture. A lively debate ensued in which many of the play's themes were identified — issues relating to colonialism, how class and culture formed the way you thought, the rights and wrongs of punishment (the condemned Liz Morden's speech had affected some of them deeply), the power relationship between the male officers and the female prisoners.

As the issues emerged, the teacher wrote them for reference on a board on the wall of the studio. She then divided the students into four groups and gave them short, photocopied sections of the play to look at. The sections were all from scenes where the convicts audition and rehearse, chosen by the teacher because they touched on something of the nature of theatre itself. With a little juggling each group was able to cast their short script, elect a director and start rehearsing. The copies of *The Recruiting Officer* provided them with the lines of the play-within-the-play which could be legitimately read, but the learning of the other lines was set as a homework task. The teacher reminded the students that serious acting invariably involved the learning of parts early on in rehearsals, and explained that in this particular play the distinction had to be clearly made between the convicts' natural speech and Farquhar's dialogue.

The following week, rehearsals continued. The teacher moved from group to group as the students struggled with their interpretations. With the memory of the professional production in mind they were keen to get things right. Information in the form of books and pictures about the eighteenth-century theatre was at hand — the teacher had mounted a display on the studio wall — and the students playing Sideway found the material on Garrick particularly helpful. From time to time, groups showed their 'work in progress' to each other and used the advice of their audiences to refine their play making.

By now, after over a year in their drama option, these students were used to seeing the studio as a kind of laboratory for experimenting with drama. Although they performed frequently, they knew that the studio was a protected environment in which the taking of risks and the stretching of possibilities was encouraged. The final presentations reflected this confidence. The short extracts were well-prepared, subtle and sometimes very funny. Above all, the teacher noticed how the students seemed to capture completely the infectious enthusiasm for drama which, in the play, drives the convict production of *The Recruiting Officer* forward against such desperate odds. The teacher ended the practical work by herself directing a dramatized reading of the final scene.

In a closing discussion, it became clear that the students were much affected by the play and impressed by the way it seemed to work so well on so many different levels. All remarked how much they had identified with the convicts.

Finally, the teacher asked the students to choose some lines from the extracts they had been working on which they thought said most about drama. Several picked Arscott's speech ...

Arscott: I don't want to play myself. When I say Kite's lines I forget everything. I forget the judge said I'm going to have to spend the rest of my natural life in this place ... I don't have to remember the things that I've done, when I speak Kite's lines I don't hate any more. I'm Kite, I'm in Shrewsbury. Can we get on with the scene, Lieutenant, and stop talking?[20]

Others remembered Dabby and Wisehammer ...

Dabby: I want to see a play that shows life as we know it.

Wisehammer: A play should make you understand something new. If it tells you what you

	already know, you leave it as ignorant as you went in.
Dabby:	Why can't we do a play about now?
Wisehammer:	It doesn't matter when a play is set. It's better if it's set in the past, it's clearer. It's easier to understand Plume and Brazen than some of the officers we know here.[21]

Others still, those who had been most moved by Sideway's dogged dedication to all things theatrical, chose . . .

Sideway:	I'm going to start a theatre company. Who wants to be in it?
Wisehammer:	I will write you a play about justice.
Sideway:	Only comedies, my boy, only comedies . . .
Liz:	I'll be in your company, Mr. Sideway.
Ketch:	And so will I. I'll play all the parts that have dignity and gravity.
Sideway:	I'll hold auditions tomorrow.[22]

For a last homework task, the students took the lines they had chosen as epigrams for reflective appreciations of the whole project. Well accustomed to using their drama notebooks for this kind of task (they had the headings in this chapter to work to) they also knew that their thoughts and feelings about *Our Country's Good* were acceptable as tapes, drawings, or poems as well as critical essays.

There is a short, unrehearsed epilogue. At the end of the lesson, three students approached the teacher with their rather dog-eared copies of *The Recruiting Officer*. 'Do you want these scripts back, Miss?' asked one.

'You see,' said another, 'we wondered . . .'

'We wondered,' said the third, 'if we could put it on, like the convicts, you know, a proper production.'

And so, from some modest acts of aesthetic recognition, the Sideway Theatre Company was born.

Notes and References

1 Barthes, R. (1977) 'The Death of the author' in *Image-music-text* (translated by Stephen Heath), London, Fontana, p. 148.
2 'Anyone under the age of 30 has basically got a cinematic eye. They're used to watching a quick succession of images; they understand visual shorthand including close-up and flash-back to point of view; it's quite different to the vocabulary of fifty years ago.' Annabel Arden, co-founder *Theatre de Complicité*, quoted in *New Statesman and Society*, 24 November 1989.
3 '... in every human language there are rules ... man cannot call the dog once dog and once cat, or utter sounds to which a consensus of people has not assigned a definite meaning ...'. Eco, U. (1983) *The Name of the Rose* (translated by William Weaver), London, Secker and Warburg.
4 Miller, J. (1986) *Subsequent Performances*, London, Faber and Faber, pp. 60–61. 'Frame' here should not be misread as 'proscenium arch'. As Miller points out, both 'a thrust stage and theatre in the round provide the spectator with implicit frames separating the two domains'.
5 See Esslin, M. (1987) *The Field of Drama*, London, Methuen, p. 38. 'Anything that is perceived on a stage — or screen — by that very fact proclaims itself as being on exhibition, being pregnant with significance ...'
6 I have been much influenced here by the work of the theatre semiotician Patrice Pavis, whose model for analyzing stage performance I have loosely adapted. This model was devised by Pavis to help drama students at the Institute of Theatre Studies at the New Sorbonne (who had no particular knowledge of semiology) to identify aspects of theatre performance for interpretation and analysis. The Pavis model is reproduced in Hornbrook, D. (1989) *Education and Dramatic Art*, Oxford, Basil Blackwell, pp. 162–3. See also Pavis, P. (1985) 'Theatre analysis: Some questions and a questionnaire', in *New Theatre Quarterly* No. 2 p. 209. For further reading, see Pavis, P. (1982) *Languages of the Stage:*

Essays in the Semiology of the Theatre, New York, Performing Arts Journal Publications.

7   Brecht, B. (1965) *The Messingkauf Dialogues*, London, Methuen, p. 86.

8   See Green, M. (1970) *The Art of Coarse Acting*, London, Arrow Books, p. 96.

9   Irving in *The Bells*, as seen by the Victorian drama critic Clement Scott. Rowell, G. (1971) *Victorian Dramatic Criticism*, London, Methuen, pp. 113–4.

10 I examine the question of inter-subjectivity and judgment in more detail in Hornbrook, D. (1989) *op. cit.*, ch. 11.

11 See Abbs, P. (Ed.) *Living Powers: the Arts in Education*, London, Falmer Press, pp. 56–62 and National Curriculum Council (Arts in Schools Project) (1990b) *The Arts 5–16: A Curriculum Framework*, Harlow, Oliver and Boyd, ch. 5.

12 The interim reports of the National Curriculum Music and Physical Education Working Groups were published in February 1991. The Music Group identified four areas of attainment in music — performing, composing, listening, knowing — while the Physical Education Group (incorporating dance) opted for three — planning and composing, participating and performing, appreciating and evaluating. See: Department of Education and Science (1991) *National Curriculum Music Working Group Interim Report*, HMSO, and Department of Education and Science (1991) *National Curriculum Physical Education Working Group Interim Report*, HMSO.

13 Peter Abbs has argued persuasively that English itself should be part of the arts curriculum. See Abbs, P. (1982) *English Within the Arts*, London, Hodder and Stoughton.

14 Fischer, E. (1963) *The Necessity of Art: A Marxist Approach*, Harmondsworth, Penguin Books, p. 152.

15 Peter Roberts' review of Brook's *Midsummer Night's Dream*, in *Plays and Players*, October 1970, p. 43.

16 *The Nativity* is the first part of a compilation based upon the York, Wakefield, Chester and Coventry cycles of Mystery Plays, which Tony Harrison wrote with the Cottesloe

Company at the National Theatre. See Harrison, T. (1985) *The Mysteries*, London, Faber and Faber.

17 *Ibid.*

18 Wertenbaker, T. (1988) *Our Country's Good*, London, Methuen. *Our Country's Good*, which is about convicts from the First Fleet putting on a production of George Farquhar's Restoration comedy, *The Recruiting Officer*, was premièred at the Royal Court Theatre in 1988, to much critical acclaim.

19 *Ibid.*, Act I, scene 2.

20 *Ibid.*, Act II, scene 7.

21 *Ibid.*

22 *Ibid.*, Act II, scene 11.

Chapter 6

Progression and Achievement

> We would stress ... that the inclusion of drama methods
> in English should not in any way replace drama as a
> subject for specialist study.
>
> *The Cox Report*, 1989[1]

Getting Better at Drama

If drama is to assume its legitimate place among the arts in
education then the question of assessment has to be addressed.
At a most fundamental level, we have to decide what achievement in drama might look like.

In the past, drama's close association with English and its
claims as a form of pedagogy have led to some confusion about
what assessing drama actually means. For diehard progressivists,
the whole idea of assessment in what they regard as a purely
subjective area of experience remains a nonsense, but the dilemma which arises from characterizing drama primarily as a learning medium raises another problem — if students are expected
to learn *through* drama, then the subject of assessment must
surely be that which they learn rather than the drama itself.

Research suggests that in recent years drama teachers have
certainly tended to incorporate personal and social as well as
specifically dramatic aims in their assessment schemes. With its

125

ease of access and flexibility, improvization has been an ideal vehicle for this compromise. Groups of children improvise around an idea and their engagement in this process then forms the basis of assessment. The originality of the idea, the social skills of the participants and their degree of commitment, the quality of the finished product and the comments made about it may all be taken into account.

General Certificate of Secondary Education (GCSE) Drama examination syllabuses in England and Wales have tended to reflect a tension between this popular and pervasive model of classroom evaluation and the demands of examination boards for some less ephemeral evidence of achievement. Thus, while an analysis by Andy Kempe of GCSE syllabuses reveals three areas of assessment common to all syllabuses — personal, social and moral, and theatrical — most syllabuses require quantities of supporting written coursework.[2] After all, it has never been reliably shown that the social skills demonstrated in drama are the *result* of engagement in drama, nor that they are necessarily sustained beyond the classroom; as Kempe points out, the fact that students pool their resources in a drama lesson is no guarantee that they will do so elsewhere. Similarly, there is no saying whether students really subscribe to the ideals they so movingly portray in a 'polished' improvization. Reliable evidence of personal and social development turns out to be very hard indeed to identify, so when it comes to examination the laudable personal and social ends of drama tend to be displaced by more tangible assessment criteria. Kempe's conclusion is that all drama syllabuses can accurately assess about candidates is 'how good they are at drama.'[3]

It might with justification be said that personal and social development should be counted as a desirable outcome of *all* education. Because the arts can so powerfully engage our cultural sensibility, it is true that some of our most profound thoughts and feelings about who we are and how we relate to others in the world may be stirred by them. However, whether this experience is necessarily developmental in any broadly humanistic sense is arguable. Many respected and successful artists (actors and playwrights among them) have been splendidly lacking in what we now rather limply call 'life skills'. Neither, as history has often tragically demonstrated, can an individual's love of the arts, however genuine, stand as guarantor for that individual's humanity. The writing of assessment programmes based upon such intangible developmental aims would be fraught with difficulty inside or outside the context of drama education.

Even if we discount such generalized ends from our considerations, other problems remain. It has been reasonably argued, for example, that progression in an arts subject cannot be compared with progression in, say, mathematics, and that existing schemes of assessment are simply inappropriate when we come to look at drama, music, dance and visual art. For one thing, what may seem 'natural' development may, in fact, be heavily culturally influenced. Also, as the National Curriculum Council Arts in Schools Project points out, a child of 8 'may be capable of insights and qualities of work which are beyond the reach of an adolescent or adult.[4] 'Getting better at drama' is clearly not a straight forward, age-related process. Finally, there is an understandable fear that any assessment programme may distort the curriculum as it will tend to concentrate on those aspects of a discipline which most readily present themselves for assessment.

Despite these difficulties — and I do not wish to underestimate them — there are increasing demands from outside to produce coherent, subject-based, assessment schemes.[5] For all its lack of foundation status, the national curriculum inevitably puts pressure on drama to bring its assessment procedures in line with those of other subjects. If drama is to retain its integrity outside English then we must establish more precisely what we mean when we speak of 'being good at drama' and what our reasonable expectations of student achievement might be.[6]

First, it is clear that we continue to make judgments about the arts on a daily basis, and that these judgments are guided by well-established, tacit criteria (that is, they are not simply arbitrary or subjective). I would therefore begin by agreeing with the Arts in Schools Project that assessment in the arts is both possible and necessary and that properly structured and shared it can actually make a positive contribution to arts education.

Effective teachers of the arts are assessing pupils' work all of the time, otherwise they would not be in a position to help them move forward. The task is to make the processes of assessment explicit and coherent.[7]

For it to be of practical use to teachers in England and Wales, however, any assessment scheme for drama must also take account of the assessment arrangements of the national curriculum. Here, attainment targets are set for knowledge, understanding, skills and aptitudes — what students know, understand and are able to do. Again, the Arts in Schools Project argues persuasively that the criterion-referenced schemes of the national curriculum — 'assessment methods based upon individual performance against agreed criteria' — are very much preferable to the practice of norm-referencing (comparing students' attainments against each other).[8] The Project's Report contains a coherent framework for assessment, based upon the two forms of activity identified as characterizing engagement in the arts — making and appraising. (For the scheme in detail, see appendix 1)[9]

How might we apply some of these ideas to drama? We have in the framework for dramatic art (see figure 1) a structure which already relates closely to the Arts in Schools model and within which indicators of progression and achievement will be easier to identify than through the traditionally more open-ended outcomes of drama-in-education. Students' abilities in production and reception will not always be unequivocally apparent, but in the end they are no less tangible than those exhibiting themselves in music and art.

In the framework for dramatic art, production is composed of making and performing plays. The *making* of plays, in various guises, actually already figures in most drama assessment schemes. Drama teachers would reasonably expect success in this area to require a combination of good ideas, knowledge of possible forms, suitable theatre skills and, generally productive group dynamics. In view of the emphasis often placed upon them, however, we should remember that the absence of the latter may not always result in poor work; there is no necessary equation between good art and comradeship. Although healthy group relations are obviously desirable, in themselves they do not satisfy the criterion of being subject specific to drama. For this reason, a generalized statement like 'awareness of and sensitivity to the group' cannot be included as a drama aptitude.[10] Also, we should not forget that some students would rather write plays than take part in improvizations. While much work in drama is naturally social, there are times when students are most productive working by themselves. This should be acknowledged in any assessment scheme, as should the contributions made to a successful production by student writers, directors, stage-managers, designers, and so on.

When it comes to the *performing* of plays, although drama teachers (along with drama examiners and moderators) are accustomed to grading performance as part of an overall assessment scheme, there remains, as we have seen, some quite deeply-rooted apprehension about students performing. I have suggested that this might in part be a concern that exposure to an audience may inhibit the natural spontaneity of students' drama, in part a fear of students affecting a shallow and indulgent 'staginess'. Given the right circumstances, however, students of all ages rise to the challenge of performance, whether it be as dancers, musicians or actors. We should not be afraid to acknowledge, therefore, that performing is as important in drama as it is for dance and music. Again, I should emphasize that there are many ways of contributing to a performance which do not involve acting. A performance assessment scheme should cover the development of technical and 'backstage' skills, such as lighting and sound operation and stage-management.

Reception complements production in the framework for dramatic art. If *audience response* is to be fully integrated into the dramatic curriculum, students will need a critical, contextualizing vocabulary which they can apply to all the performances they see or in which they take part. This vocabulary will enable students to communicate their dramatic knowledge and understanding and help them to place their experience of drama in a wider cultural context. HMI suggest that such a vocabulary should include:

... knowledge of the place and purposes of drama in society; of the beginnings of drama and its links with religion; of a range of forms of drama and theatre and their conventions; of the theatre as a place of work and cultural influence; of the contribution of the arts to the wealth of a country; of the educational uses of drama and theatre.[11]

With a growing background of contextual knowledge students should be able to refine their ability to respond to the dramas they see with increasingly well-informed judgment. An assessment scheme for reception, or responding, should take account both of the knowledge and understanding students are able to demonstrate and their ability to use that vocabulary to interpret what they see and hear. As I hope the examples in this book indicate, students can be introduced to drama from a variety of historical and cultural sources so that their theatrical experience grows naturally in breadth and diversity as they progress through the dramatic curriculum.

In practice, production and reception in drama are interdependent; the emphasis placed on each will vary across the dramatic curriculum as teachers make choices about what they teach and the material they use. However, the principle of balance is most important. The dramatic curriculum should not be allowed to become lopsided with too much attention being paid to one aspect at the expense of others. Education in drama should offer the same synthesis of skills, understanding and knowledge that might be expected of any other arts subject.

We may now bring these thoughts about assessment together in the form of three key statements. These statements mark out the parameters of attainment and will form the basis of an assessment scheme for drama.

Production
Making plays — the development of students' ability to manipulate dramatic form in order to interpret and express ideas;
Performing plays — the development of students' capacity to participate in dramatic presentations.

Reception
Responding to plays — the development of students' ability
    to make informed and discerning judgements about the
    dramas they see or in which they participate.[12]

Any programme of assessment must be coherent, compati-
ble (with other schemes, in effect, in England and Wales, with
the national curriculum arrangements) and easy to use. This
means that in drama we too will be concerned with knowledge,
understanding, skills and aptitudes (and not with potentially
controversial intangibles like attitudes), that what we assess
must be realistically measurable (excluding imprecise targets
like, 'the ability to engage with drama at a feeling level') and
that all we propose must relate to paths of progression which
students can understand. Above all, if we are to maintain the
independence of dramatic art, all attainment in drama must be
subject specific — it must represent achievement *in drama*.
    The proposals which follow acknowledge the assessment
principles laid out in the report of the National Curriculum Task
Group on Assessment and Testing (TGAT).[13] The arrangement
of Key Stages and Levels recommended by the report will be
familiar to teachers in England and Wales, and those wishing to
be reminded of it may turn to appendix 2. For the benefit of
non-initiates, in what follows I have attempted to simplify the
national curriculum arrangements by referring to the ages of
students rather than the levels of attainment. However, because
progression in the arts is not necessarily linear — 'children do
not become more skilful and knowledgeable in the arts simply
by getting older'[14] — and because students will vary greatly in
their rates of maturation, the age-linking of attainment I have
indicated should be taken very broadly and with all the reservations indicated above.
    In order to achieve some comparability with existing statu-
tory Orders and with advice from HMI, reference is made to the
Levels of Attainment spelt out in the Order for English in the
National Curriculum and to those recommended in HMI's *Drama from 5 to 16*. Otherwise, the indication of levels that follows
simply represents what I believe the majority of students to be
capable of.

Mapping Progression — Production

Making plays — the development of students' ability to
  manipulate dramatic form in order to interpret and
  express ideas;
Performing plays — the development of students' capacity
  to participate in dramatic presentations.

With very young children it is not always easy to make distinctions between play and drama. However, 7-year-olds in English are expected to be able to 'participate as speakers and listeners in group activities, including imaginative play', for example by playing a 'shopkeeper or customer in the class shop.'[15] HMI consider that by the age of 7 children should be able to identify with the characters and actions of a dramatized story.[16]

On the whole, students of primary age need little encouragement to take advantage of opportunities to improvize and act out plays in the classroom. Even by the age of 7 most children have developed an understanding of dramatic narrative and can render quite sophisticated dramatized accounts of stories they know or have invented. As HMI point out, clothes and properties, well-chosen stories and poems, puppets and musical instruments, are invaluable additional stimuli in drama for younger students.[17]

By the age of 10 or 11 in English, most students are expected to be able to participate in the presentation of a story or scene of their own devising.[18] In drama, participation can be developed to involve small groups of students improvising scenes and using a range of dramatic techniques — mime, masks, music, dance — to tell a story. At this age particularly, the use of mime and dance can be a way of enabling less vocally extrovert students to play significant parts.

Teachers should not be afraid of introducing 9-year-olds to scripts, particularly in the form of extracts. Where these relate to themes already improvized they can help to refine students' dramatic experience and lead to a more precise use of language. Also at this age, students should be encouraged to notate their work where appropriate. Notation should start from simple scenarios, or lists of scenes and events, but students with a facility for writing should be encouraged to attempt scripted dialogue. In English, most 9-year-olds will be writing stories 'with detail beyond simple events and with a defined ending.'[19]

When assessing work in drama, the primary teacher may not wish to distinguish too rigidly between attainment in drama and other learning outcomes, particularly, perhaps, those coming under English in the national curriculum. However, in the primary school the foundations are being laid for drama in subsequent years, and it is important that attention is paid to the dramatic form in which students express their ideas as well as to the ideas themselves. By restricting students to the use of mime, or obliging them to include specific incidents or characters, or by making a narrator a requirement, students are helped to extend their understanding of dramatic form beyond simple naturalism and melodrama.

Opportunities for performance are usually plentiful in the primary school. Events on the Christian and non-Christian religious calendar, for example, are often times when groups of students can prepare plays for assembly or for visiting parents, and classes will sometimes take it in turn to perform dramatic work to the rest of the school. These occasions are not only an important part of the communal life of the school but also a valuable element of the dramatic curriculum.

Among other things, HMI believe that by the age of 11 in drama most students should be able to make and take part in improvised scenes and act out convincing characters. They should also have developed sufficient physical flexibility to enable them to adapt voice and movement in a controlled manner to the characters they play.

By this age, students should have grasped the principles which govern the creation of a dramatic environment and be aware of the potential use of design and technology in drama. In the words of HMI, they should be able to 'deploy physical materials, colour, light and sound to create a space for drama'.[20]

At 11, most students in drama should be able to expand scenarios into simple dramatic scripts (in English, playscripts are specifically mentioned as an example of an appropriate activity for students working to level 5).[21] By the time they leave the primary school, all students should know how to polish their work for presentation and should have become accustomed to the disciplines of rehearsal and to the process of refining their plays in the light of audience response.

The first year of the secondary school should be a time when drama teachers challenge their new students with a range of diverse dramatic forms and encourage them to incorporate this widening frame of reference in their play making. By the age of 14, students should be comfortable experimenting with all kinds of different styles and should be able to produce original texts which are themselves innovative and challenging. At the same time, work on scripts, initiated in the primary school, should be developed and extended. Students of 12 and 13 should already be graduating from extracts to short scripted plays, and by the age of 14 groups of students should feel confident about taking up an unfamiliar script, rehearsing it and performing it to their peers.

As performers, students of 15 and 16 should be able to employ distinct acting styles and use devices like comic timing to good effect. HMI suggest that by the age of 16, students should be able to 'call upon a range of subtle skills in voice, posture, movement and gesture in order to sustain and develop dramatic action.'[22] These physical skills should be complemented with the sensitivity and insight necessary to sustain rounded and believable characters in performance.

Notation should be a regular feature of the dramatic curriculum throughout the secondary school; 14-year-olds should be able to notate their work in such a way that it can be reproduced as a dramatic text by others. The statutory Order for English (Writing) gives an indication of the degree of sophistication which might be reasonably expected at different levels.

Students making plays in the secondary school should increasingly demonstrate an understanding of the contribution that design and technology can make to production. Sets, costumes and properties, however simple, should be regularly incorporated into play making by the age of 14, and wherever possible, students should use stage lighting to enhance their work. HMI believe that at 16, students 'should be able to integrate sound and silence, movement and stillness, light and darkness to make effective use of spaces where dramatic action

takes place.'[23] Lighting control and sound mixing, as well as
slides and video, are all technical devices with which students
studying drama at this level should be familiar.

By the age of 16, students should be able to produce dramatic texts which are entertaining and thought-provoking for an
adult audience. Brecht reminded us that 'the contrast between
learning and amusing oneself is not laid down by any divine
rule,'[24] and although at this level play making should have an
underlying seriousness of purpose, we should not necessarily
expect from our students plays loaded to the gunwales with
meaningful issues. Being able to make an audience laugh at the
right moments also represents attainment in drama. 16-year-olds
studying drama should have had the experience of performing in
a variety of formal and informal situations and should be familiar with what HMI describe as 'the organization, discipline and
teamwork necessary to perform drama to others.'[25]

Drama notebooks should form part of the process of assessment in the secondary school. These need not be seen as a chore,
but as an opportunity for the collation of material associated
with students' play making and performance. Cartoons of
dramatic stories, expressions of their thoughts in pictures, prose
or poetry, design ideas, collections of suitable music on tape or
photographs encapsulating moments they wish to portray — all
may be included. Because of the ephemeral nature of the performing arts, records of this kind will be useful *aide-mémoires* for
the students themselves as well as providing important back-up
evidence for teacher assessment.

Mapping Progression — Reception

Responding to plays — the development of students' ability
to make informed and discerning judgments about the
dramas they see or in which they participate.

I have suggested that the question that might be asked of any
dramatic piece is, 'How well does it convey what is intended?' A
comic routine which does not make us laugh or an adventure
story which we cannot follow are simple examples of a failure to

communicate to an audience. Even very young children implicitly address this in their dramatic play. The infant who says,
'No, the *princess* should have the crown', has made a critical
judgment of the way the meaning of the play is being communicated. All work on reception should start from an examination
of this simple question.

At the age of 7, students are quite capable of commenting
about the dramas they see. In English, 8 and 9-year-olds should
be able to 'listen attentively to stories, talk about setting, story
line and characters and recall significant details.'[26] The same
applies to drama. All primary students should be encouraged to
discuss their experience of watching drama, for example after a
performance by another class, and to express opinions about the
form and content of plays. At the same time, the positive
attitude to dramatic work reflected in the assessments of a good
teacher should be encouraged in students' own critical approach
from an early age. Students should learn to approach a drama
with minds open enough to perceive its qualities, however few.

From early in the primary school, students should realize
that there is a language of dramatic convention. The primary
dramatic curriculum should then be designed to provide opportunities for them progressively to acquire a dramatic vocabulary.
Infants should be able to recognize the difference between telling
a story and acting it and between reality and dramatized versions
of it. By the time they are 7, students should know the essential
features which distinguish drama from other forms of human
expression and realize that there is a link between the dramas
they make in the classroom and those they watch on television
or when theatre companies visit the school. By the age of 9 or
10, students should be able to grasp the basic ingredients of
dramatic narrative — tension, conflict, surprise, plot development and resolution — and have a fair idea of drama's historical
and cultural diversity. By 11, students should have been introduced to basic dramatic forms, such as comedy, tragedy and
farce, as well as to a variety of European and non-European
theatre styles, and should be able to recognize these forms and
styles when confronted by them.

In English, students of 8 and 9 are expected to be able to
'read aloud from familiar stories and poems fluently and with

appropriate expression.'[27] Students of this age should also be reading scripts and know the conventions which distinguish playscripts from other literary forms. They should understand how the words on the page notate live action, how scripts become performances and how dramatic productions are rehearsed and presented.

Students should complete their primary education in drama with the ability to offer (and receive) criticism constructively and to place their judgments in the context of a growing framework of dramatic reference. HMI consider that students of this age should be able to 'recognise good work in drama through a detailed and critical observation of the characters created, the issues involved and the processes employed.'[28]

From the age of 11 onwards a systematic approach to dramatic appreciation should be incorporated into the dramatic curriculum, based, perhaps, on the model in Chapter 5. As they progress through the secondary drama curriculum, students should be able to make increasingly perceptive responses to their own work and that of others. They should also be able to contextualize their play making and performance within a growing knowledge of professional productions, theatrical forms and dramatic literature.

In the first year of secondary school, students should be introduced to the idea that drama, like all the arts, may be more than a straightforward expression of intention. As well as looking at links across the arts, they should be beginning to understand the pervasiveness of drama in the world about them. The drama of everyday life (social-texts) and television drama (electronic-texts) should be part of the discourse of drama lessons from the ages of 12 and 13.

By the age of 14, students should be taking account of dramatic pieces as representatives of specific genres — pantomime, verse drama, and so on — and be looking for the imaginative and interesting treatment of themes in the plays they see. They should be considering how ideas and issues are interpreted through drama and how scripts are realized by directors, designers and actors. When they watch a drama they should recognize that, in the words of HMI, 'there may be alternative interpretations of dramatic meaning which have equal validity.'[29] 14-year-olds visiting the theatre should be able to respond to the performance as a whole as well as identify key elements for analysis and subsequent discussion.[30]

Every opportunity should be taken for students to gain experience of the professional theatre. This may be achieved by having companies perform in the school or by organizing visits to see plays outside. The secondary drama curriculum should enable students to learn all they can about the practical business of the theatre; visits backstage and opportunities to interview actors and other theatre workers should be arranged whenever possible. By 14, students should know how a professional theatre company works and be able to describe the contributions made by directors, playwrights, stage-managers, and so on, to a professional production.

By the age of 16, students should have developed a solid foundation of theatrical reference to guide them in their own dramatic work and against which they can measure new experiences. In English, 16-year-olds are expected to be able to 'read a range of fiction, poetry, literary non-fiction and drama, including pre-20th century literature.'[31] Drama students following option courses at this level should have a working knowledge of key plays from the European tradition — that is, from Classical Greece, the Middle Ages, the Elizabethan period, the Restoration, the nineteenth and twentieth centuries — and this should be complemented by acquaintance with traditional non-European forms such as the Noh Theatre of Japan or the Hindu drama of India. Students should always understand the historical and cultural context of the drama and be given the opportunity to work practically with examples.

In responding to performances, students at this level should be able to deliver constructive criticism which takes full account of the practical circumstances of a particular production. They should understand how groups are funded and be aware of the financial restrictions on many companies and how that may affect their work. Similarly, their knowledge of production practicalities, such as touring a small production and setting up in school halls, should inform their comments about staging and other technical matters.

Students' ability to respond to and learn from what they see will often be most accurately reflected in their production work. In practice, therefore, teachers should not seek to partition these two elements of the dramatic curriculum. Assessment processes should acknowledge that there is probably no better way of determining the quality of students' response to drama than when its results are manifest in their own productions. At the same time, first hand, practical experience of making and performing plays will help to temper and inform the appraisals students make of the plays they see.

Levels of Attainment in Drama

For the final part of this chapter, I have taken the framework for 'Attainment targets and associated statements of attainment' used for national curriculum subjects, and projected upon it some statements of attainment in drama based on the maps of progression in production and reception outlined above. Employing national curriculum terminology, under such a scheme, *Production* and *Reception* translate into Profile Components. *Making*, *Performing* and *Responding* thus become the three Attainment Targets for drama.

The point of this exercise is to show how it is just as possible to identify progression and achievement in drama as it is in art, music or any other subject. However, the levels of attainment indicated here are not intended for slavish adherence but rather as benchmarks for the assessment of drama in primary and secondary schools. As much practical work in drama integrates the making and performing of plays in the form of improvization, particularly for younger students, teachers may wish to pull the first two Attainment Targets — Making and Performing — into one and assess work under a single Profile Component — Production. Similarly, teachers will probably wish to emphasize different aspects of drama at different points in the dramatic curriculum; there is no suggestion that all the areas of attainment should be tackled all the time.

Rather than differentiate minutely between each level, I have followed the terms of reference of the Music and Art Working Groups and attempted to give a broad picture of progression in drama by picking four points on the scale relating to the four key stages of the national curriculum (see appendix 2). Thus, the statements of attainment that follow broadly represent what students 'of different abilities and maturities' can be expected to achieve in drama at the end of each key stage.

I have, however, made an exception at key stage 4. Here, rather than indicating average achievement, I have chosen to indicate attainment at level 10 on the grounds that this may fairly be taken to be equivalent to an A grade at GCSE. The proposed attainment levels at key stage 4 thus represent the peak of achievement in the 7 to 16 dramatic curriculum.

ATTAINMENT TARGETS AND ASSOCIATED STATEMENTS OF ATTAINMENT IN DRAMA: KEY STAGES 1 TO 4.

Attainment Target 1: Making

● ●

The development of students' ability to manipulate dramatic form in order to interpret and express ideas.

STATEMENTS OF ATTAINMENT	EXAMPLE
At the end of key stage 1 (age 7), students should be able to:	
a) participate inventively in make-believe play.	*Become practically absorbed in the spontaneous enactment of a story; use their ideas to move the story along.*
b) sustain dramatic play to a satisfying conclusion.	*Pursue a piece of make-believe so that it has a recognizable 'ending'.*

STATEMENTS OF ATTAINMENT	EXAMPLE
c) maintain narrative consistency within a dramatic improvization.	*Act out a simple story with clearly delineated characters and plot.*

At the end of key stage 2 (age 11), students should be able to:

a) contribute imaginatively, as a member of a group, to the making of a rehearsed dramatic scene.	*Help with ideas for a classroom improvization on a given theme.*
b) show in their play making that they can structure coherent dramatic narratives.	*Devise dramas which have 'a beginning, a middle and an end', and which sustain the interest of an audience.*
c) incorporate a choice of dramatic techniques and conventions in their play making.	*Employ the device of the narrator; use music or dance.*
d) read familiar playscripts and understand how stage directions are used.	*Guide other students through a dramatized reading of a play.*
e) demonstrate an understanding of how dramatic action is framed in performance.	*Suggest simple stage settings appropriate to a class play; arrange furniture and other items to establish a suitable environment for an improvization.*

STATEMENTS OF ATTAINMENT	EXAMPLE

At the end of key stage 3 (age 14), students should be able to:

a) engage fully in the production process and use all its basic elements to follow through their ideas to a satisfactory conclusion.

Resolve difficulties encountered during the devising process; take part in rehearsals with commitment; edit 'work-in-progress' in the light of informed response; complete the drama in a form ready for showing.

b) demonstrate the use of a wide variety of dramatic forms and techniques and incorporate them into their dramas.

Deploy mime, tableaux, and storytelling techniques with confidence; use flash-back in a dramatic narrative.

c) read from an increasingly wide range of playscripts and visualize them in production.

Sketch designs for a production of a play with which they are not familiar; present a performance of a short extract from a published play to a group of peers.

d) notate their work in the form of written scripts.

Write down a group-devised play so that it can be rehearsed and performed by others.

e) organize, dress and light a dramatic space imaginatively and show an understanding of how stage artefacts may be used symbolically.

Design a simple set and realize it in the available space; use lighting and costumes to help signify the themes of a drama.

STATEMENTS OF ATTAINMENT	EXAMPLE
At the end of key stage 4 (age 16), students at level 10 should be able to:	
a) experiment with unorthodox dramatic approaches to material to produce dramas which are thought-provoking and original.	*Consciously challenge the conventions of naturalism with the use of mask; use Brechtian 'alienation' techniques.*
b) devise dramas which display a grasp of dramatic tension, focus and narrative development in the coherent presentation of a theme to an adult audience.	*Incorporate the conventions of exposition, complication, crisis and denouement.*
c) introduce elements of allegory, ambiguity, dissonance, irony and metaphor into their play making.	*Write, rehearse and perform a short allegorical play to a group of peers.*
d) interpret in performance a range of dramatic scripts.	*Recognize the dramatic potential of an unfamiliar play script and direct it in rehearsal.*
e) demonstrate how set and costume design, lighting, sound and other technical effects can be integrated into a dramatic piece.	*Make and use a set design and model; show where lights should be placed to achieve particular effects; prepare a sound effects tape.*

Attainment Target 2: Performing

● ●

The development of students' capacity to participate in dramatic presentations.

STATEMENTS OF ATTAINMENT	EXAMPLE
At the end of key stage 1 (age 7), students should be able to:	
a) consciously empathize with the characters and roles chosen.	*Play the part of a character in a story with some consistency and commitment.*

At the end of key stage 2 (age 11), students should be able to:	
a) invent and sustain interesting and convincing roles in a drama.	*Play a convincing part in an improvization which fits in with the story and which is consistent.*
b) adapt voice and movement to the demands of a chosen role or character.	*Show that they can control their movement to portray characters older than themselves.*

145

STATEMENTS OF ATTAINMENT	EXAMPLE
c) perform confidently as a member of a group to peers and selected adults.	*Show their work in the school assembly, or to an audience of parents.*
d) carry out appropriate 'back-stage' tasks during a performance.	*Organize the properties for a class play.*

At the end of key stage 3 (age 14), students should be able to:

a) show evidence of being able to sustain dramatic roles of some depth.	*Portray rounded, three-dimensional characters with conviction.*
b) employ vocal and movement skills to portray convincingly a range of different characters.	*Switch smoothly from narrator to character while telling a story.*
c) adapt themselves as performers to a variety of dramatic roles and demonstrate a grasp of performance technique.	*Play parts in scripted and improvized productions which show range and flexibility; use dramatic pause or comic timing effectively.*
d) demonstrate the use of lighting and sound equipment and show how productions are cued and managed.	*Stage-manage or operate the sound or lighting for a class play.*

STATEMENTS OF ATTAINMENT	EXAMPLE
At the end of key stage 4 (age 16), students at level 10 should be able to:	
a) employ a range of emotional reference to create, develop and sustain three-dimensional dramatic characters.	*Use Stanislavskian techniques to build a character; sustain a convincing role in an extended improvization.*
b) utilize a range of 'subtle skills in voice, posture, movement and gesture' in order to develop and portray different characters.[32]	*Create spontaneously a variety of convincing roles; interpret with confidence a major character from a published play.*
c) perform, as a member of a group, to a variety of different audiences.	*Participate in a devised performance for a local primary school; take a substantial part in the school play or local youth theatre production.*
d) take responsibility for an aspect of the back-stage or technical operation of a public performance.	*Cue a youth theatre production; operate a sound desk during a school play.*

Attainment Target 3: Responding

● ●

The development of students' ability to make informed and discerning judgments about the dramas they see or in which they participate.

STATEMENTS OF ATTAINMENT	EXAMPLE
At the end of key stage 1 (age 7), students should be able to:	
a) comment constructively after dramatic play and show an interest in the dramas of others.	*Talk about what they have done and remember significant parts.*
b) show in discussion that they can distinguish between coherence and incoherence in dramatic play.	*Say when something is not being clearly portrayed.*
c) demonstrate an understanding of drama as a distinct form of human activity.	*Make comparisons between their own dramatic play and dramas they have seen on television.*

STATEMENTS OF ATTAINMENT	EXAMPLE

At the end of key stage 2 (age 11), students should be able to:

a) speak fluently, accurately and interestingly about their own and other's dramatic work.

Participate in a group discussion after the performance of a class play and contribute productive comments and opinions.

b) recognize good drama through detailed, critical observation.

Talk objectively about the characters, the action, and the treatment of issues in a performance by a young people's theatre company.

c) show that they can distinguish between different types of drama, describe the characterizing features of key forms and make connections between drama and real life.

Say how a television drama differs from a live performance; use examples to explain the difference between stage comedy and tragedy; describe an example of dramatized myth.

d) demonstrate a basic understanding of the way dramatic narratives are constructed and of the non-literal function of drama.

Identify tension, conflict, surprise and plot in a drama that they see; group performers together to represent abstract ideas, such as 'hope' or 'gratitude'.

e) show that they understand the basic elements of the production process.

Explain how a play is prepared for performance; discuss the relationship between the actors and the director.

STATEMENTS OF ATTAINMENT	EXAMPLE
At the end of key stage 3 (age 14), students should be able to:	
a) contribute, to group discussions, considered opinions or clear statements of personal feeling about a play which are also responsive to the contributions of others.[33]	*Express an initial reaction to a performance but be prepared to have it modified in the light of alternative interpretations.*
b) identify evidence of the contributions made to a performance by different members of the production team.	*Recognize how ideas and issues have been interpreted by a production; talk about the contribution of the designer or the director.*
c) discuss plays as representatives of particular genres located in cultures and history, and appreciate the many forms of dramatic representation that exist in addition to those which happen in theatres.	*Explain the characteristics of pantomime; talk about the transposition of a play by a director from one period to another; recognize and discuss some of the dramas of everyday life.*
d) demonstrate an understanding of the workings of the professional theatre and of the roles of a range of theatre workers.	*Describe the way a production team works; outline the responsibilities of the stage-manager or designer.*

STATEMENTS OF ATTAINMENT	EXAMPLE
e) appreciate the relationship between drama and the other arts.	*Discuss the contribution that can be made by music or dance to a dramatic performance.*

At the end of key stage 4 (age 16), students at level 10 should be able to:

a) express, in discussion or in writing, an informed opinion of a dramatic performance with clarity and cogency.[34]	*Write a hypothetical review for a national newspaper; present a verbal critique to a group of peers.*
b) identify the characteristics of different dramatic genres and their cultural contexts, and call upon suitable contemporary or historical examples.	*Demonstrate an understanding of the characterizing features of Shakespearean drama; discuss the use of street-theatre or spectacle in contemporary society.*
c) appreciate how the individual members of a production team contribute to the success of a dramatic performance.	*Explain how the work of the administrator of a small theatre company relates to the actors.*
d) show an understanding of how social, political and economic factors affect the production of drama and how professional theatre companies operate.	*Participate in a discussion about the funding of theatre; interpret the budget of a small theatre company and identify its financial strengths and weaknesses.*

151

STATEMENTS OF ATTAINMENT	EXAMPLE
e) describe the place of drama in society and identify and comment upon its many different manifestations.	*Discuss the influence of television drama on live theatre; suggest ways in which young people might become more involved in drama.*
f) record in a systematic way their impressions of and involvement with a range of dramatic experience.	*Compile a short documentary of video-recorded evidence of their work; keep a scrap-book of their reviews of productions.*

Notes and References

1   Department of Education and Science (1989a) *English for Ages 5 to 16 (The Cox Report)*, HMSO, para. 8.3
2   See Kempe, A. (1989) 'Towards a Common Syllabus', in *2D*, 9/1, Winter.
3   *Ibid.*
4   National Curriculum Council (Arts in Schools Project) (1990b) *The Arts 5–16: A Curriculum Framework*, Harlow, Oliver and Boyd, p. 60.
5   Not least, from the School Examinations and Assessment Council (SEAC).
6   See chapter 1, note 18.
7   National Curriculum Council (Arts in Schools Project) (1990b)
8   *Ibid.*, p. 59.
9   *Ibid.*, pp. 64–8.
10 This is not to say that the ability to work in a group should not be incorporated within a specifically drama statement. For example: 'the ability to work cooperatively in a production team'. Here, it is clearly implied that being able to 'work cooperatively' is essential for the success of the production. Similarly, 'the ability to improvize collaboratively' is as much a necessary requirement for spontaneous classroom improvization as it would be for a *commedia* troup. HMI fall into this trap when they suggest that, as a learning objective in drama, 16-year-olds should be able to 'show insight into, and sympathy for, human and cultural differences.' I would argue that while this is a highly desirable objective it is not drama specific. See Department of Education and Science (1989b) *Drama from 5 to 16: HMI Curriculum Matters 17*, HMSO, para. 13.
11 *Drama from 5 to 16, op. cit.*, para. 18.iv.
12 In the interests of cogency, this statement collapses the two Arts in Schools 'appraising' categories — critical response and contextual understanding — into one. While 'informed and discerning judgments' are not, in my view, possible without appropriate contextual knowledge, programmes of

study in drama may usefully reinstate the Arts in Schools differentiation.

13 Department of Education and Science (1988) *National Curriculum: Task Group on Assessment and Testing Report (The TGAT Report)*, London, HMSO.

14 *The Arts, 5–16, op. cit.*, p. 61.

15 Statutory Order for English, Speaking and Listening, Level 1. Department of Education and Science (1990a) *English in the National Curriculum (Statutory Order for English)*, HMSO.

16 *Drama from 5 to 16, op. cit.*, para. 11.

17 *Ibid.*, para. 33.

18 *Statutory Order for English, op. cit.*, Speaking and Listening, Level 4.

19 *Ibid.*, Writing, Level 3.

20 *Drama from 5 to 16, op. cit.*, para. 12.

21 Level 5 is intended to indicate the top of the average ability range (80 per cent of students) at age 11. See *Statutory Order for English, op. cit.*, Writing, Level 5.

22 *Drama from 5 to 16, op. cit.*, para. 13.

23 *Ibid.*

24 From Brecht, B. (1964) 'Theatre for Pleasure or Theatre for Instruction', in *Brecht on Theatre: The Development of an Aesthetic* (edited and translated by John Willett), New York, Hill and Wang, p. 72.

25 *Drama from 5 to 16, op. cit.*, para. 13.

26 *Statutory Order for English, op. cit.*, Reading, Level 3.

27 *Ibid.*

28 *Drama from 5 to 16, op. cit.*, para. 12.

29 *Ibid.*, para. 13.

30 It should be noted again that writing may not necessarily be the most appropriate medium for the expression of response, even at this stage; the attainment in drama of those for whom English is not their first language, for example, should not suffer through difficulties with written English. Drama notebooks, as recommended in this chapter, should present opportunities for art work, poetry, annotated cuttings, sound and videotapes, for example, as well as for continuous prose.

31 *Statutory Order for English, op. cit.*, Reading, Level 8.

32 See also *Drama from 5 to 16, op. cit.*, para. 13.
33 See also *ibid.*, Speaking and Listening, Level 6.
34 See also *Statutory Order for English, op. cit.*, Speaking and Listening, Level 10.

Afterpiece

Once the new way of thinking has been established, the old problems vanish; indeed they become hard to recapture. For they go with our way of expressing ourselves and, if we clothe ourselves in a new form of expression, the old problems are discarded along with the old garment.

Ludwig Wittgenstein, 1946[1]

In this book I have presented a programme for education in drama based on my belief that it is possible to reconcile membership of the wider arts community with the idea of drama as an independent educative force. By building this programme around a simple structure of production and reception which has the dramatic text at its core, and by identifying making, performing and responding to plays as the three key elements of dramatic art, I have proposed both a framework for teaching and the foundations of a dramatic curriculum.

Unfortunately, periods of rapid change provide distinctly unstable platforms from which to project any prognosis or vision of the future. (Those who were putting the finishing touches to theses about the progress of the Cold War as I began this book in the autumn of 1989 will know the truth of this only too well.) Since 1988, the Education Reform Act has ensured that education in England and Wales has been subjected to upheavals not witnessed in this country since the post-war period. The national curriculum is only one element of a comprehensive programme designed to shift fundamentally the balance of power within the education service and expose schools to the forces of the market.

However, the life expectancy of these 'reforms' is impossible to predict. As parents begin to realise the debilitating effect their imposition is having on the whole education culture, the 1988 Act may (like the Berlin Wall) turn out to be less of an impediment to progress than pessimists predict. While it is difficult to imagine a return under any government to those *laissez faire* days when politicians were content to leave 'the secret garden of the curriculum'[2] to the educational experts, even as I write substantial cracks are already appearing in the no-nonsense ten-subject edifice which was so carelessly unveiled in 1987.

For my part, although I consider the 1988 national curriculum irresponsibly ill-conceived and parochial, I am not at all ill-disposed to the idea that all young people of school age have an entitlement to a properly evaluated and balanced education. What is needed now is agreement and consensus over this entitlement rather than the debilitating cycle of dogmatic assertion and shabby compromise to which we have become accustomed.

While they might dream of better times, teachers still have to work and be effective in the world as it is. I have tried to acknowledge this in my proposals for a dramatic curriculum. At the same time, any really useful framework for drama in schools must be sustainable beyond the vagaries of political fashion. Thus, while I am aware that the minutiae of national curriculum assessment may pass into history very quickly (and will anyhow be irrelevant to readers from abroad), by making reference to them, in chapter 6 for example, my hope is that teachers will see both the immediate relevance of a national curriculum related scheme of progression and the longer term importance of establishing the *principle* of shared criteria for achievement in drama.

Above all, it is the theatre language employed throughout this book that I hope will find its way into the bloodstream of drama teaching. By introducing the vocabulary of the theatre into primary and secondary classrooms I have tried to encourage school drama out of its conceptual isolation so that it can begin

157

to share an altogether wider and more generally understood dramatic discourse. If drama teachers can learn to feel at home with the common vocabulary of actors, directors and playwrights, then this above anything else will ensure the future of education in drama. If this book goes some way towards making this eclectic end a reality, then it will have served its purpose.

Notes and References

1   Wittgenstein, L. (1980) *Culture and Value*, (edited by G.H. von Wright and translated by Peter Winch), Oxford, Basil Blackwell, p. 48e.
2   A phrase coined by David Eccles when Minister of Education in the 1960s.

Appendix 1

National Curriculum Council Arts in Schools Project: Areas for Assessment in the Arts

Making

Practical work in the arts involves the use and manipulation of media — sounds, images, movements, words — to create forms which clarify and express the artist's ideas and perceptions. There are two main areas of assessment: creative development, and technical development.

Creative Development

This area concerns the content of pupils' own work in the arts: the nature and quality of their ideas and the forms in which they express them.

- *Objective 1*
  Pupils should demonstrate the ability to use the processes of the arts to generate and explore their own ideas and perceptions.
- *Objective 2*
  Pupils should demonstrate the ability to develop and sustain their ideas and perceptions from original concept to realized form.

Technical Development

This area concerns pupils' practical skills in the use and control of the arts media, and the development of techniques in applying these skills to their own work.

- *Objective 3*
  Pupils should demonstrate the ability to control the chosen media of expression with confidence and precision.
- *Objective 4*
  Pupils should demonstrate the ability to use their practical skills appropriately within the artistic intentions of their work.

Appraising

Arts education is concerned with extending pupils' knowledge and understanding of the arts and with deepening their sensibilities to actual works. The way pupils respond is affected by their own values and attitudes and by their understanding of the cultural context within which the work was made and the intentions of the artist. There are two areas for assessment: critical response, and contextual understanding.

Critical Response

This concerns the nature of pupils' responses to, and awareness of, the qualities of existing works in the arts and their ability to describe their responses in appropriate terms.

- *Objective 5*
  Pupils should demonstrate the ability to describe significant features of their own and others' work using relevant concepts and terminology.
- *Objective 6*
  Pupils should demonstrate the ability to make informed

and discerning judgments about their own and others' work and to identify their criteria.

Contextual Understanding

This area concerns pupils' knowledge and understanding of different cultural practices and conventions in the arts.

- *Objective 7*
  Pupils should demonstrate relevant knowledge and understanding of different cultural practices and traditions in the arts.

From National Curriculum Council (Arts in Schools Project) (1990b) *The Arts 5–16: A Curriculum Framework*, Harlow, Oliver and Boyd, pp. 65–6.

Structure for Assessment in the National Curriculum: Levels of Achievement

As shown in figure 6, the assessment scheme for the national curriculum uses a scale of 1 to 10 to cover the full range of progress that students of different abilities make between the ages of 5 and 16. The numbers on the scale are known as *Levels*, each representing a criterion–based level of achievement.

Alongside each Level in every national curriculum subject (art and music are included, but not drama) are *Statements of Attainment* relating to *Attainment Targets* identified by the subject working groups. Thus, 'Writing' is an English Attainment Target with a Statement of Attainment at Level 3 requiring that students should be able to 'produce a range of types of non-chronological writing.'

A student who has mastered the understanding and competence required for attainment at Level 3 in a subject will be working to achieve the criteria contained in the Statements of Attainment for Level 4.

Any one Level represents the same competencies in the subject whatever the age of the student. In any class, some students will be at higher levels than others. The bold line in figure 6 indicates the expected results for students at the ages specified. The dotted lines represent the approximate limits within which the great majority of students should lie. Thus, nearly all 11-year-olds should fall within Levels 3, 4 and 5.

For the purposes of assessment, the years of compulsory

[handwritten margin note: The idea of mastery before going on to next. Is this contrary to a spiral curric?]

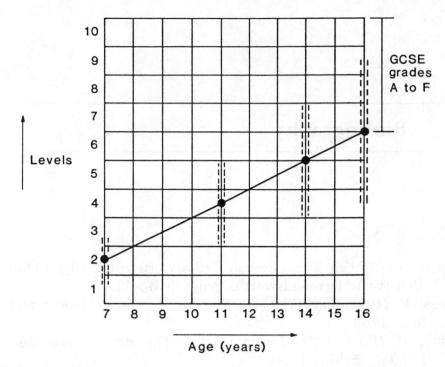

Figure 6: Sequence of student achievement of levels between ages 7 and 16.

schooling are divided into four *Key Stages*, two primary and two secondary.

Primary
Key Stage 1: 5 to 7-year-olds
Key Stage 2: 7 to 11-year-olds

Secondary
Key Stage 3: 11 to 14-year-olds
Key Stage 4: 14 to 16-year-olds (GCSE options).

See Department of Education and Science (1988), *National Curriculum: Task Group on Assessment and Testing Report (The TGAT Report)*, London, HMSO.

Bibliography

AESCHYLUS (1956) The Orestian Trilogy, (translated by Philip Vellacott) Harmondsworth, Penguin Books.

ABBS, P. (1982) *English Within the Arts*, London, Hodder and Stoughton.

ABBS, P. (Ed.) (1987) *Living Powers: The Arts in Education*, London, Falmer Press.

ABBS, P. (Ed.) (1989) *The Symbolic Order*, London, Falmer Press.

ABBS, P. and RICHARDSON, J. (1990) *The Forms of Narrative: A Practical Guide*, Cambridge, England, Cambridge University Press.

BARTHES, R. (1977) *Image — Music — Text*, (translated by Stephen Heath) London, Fontana/Collins.

BAZALGETTE, C. (Ed.) (1989) *Primary Media Education: A Curriculum Statement*, London, British Film Institute.

BENJAMIN, W. (1970) *Illuminations*, London, Fontana/Collins.

BERMAN, M. (1982) *All That Is Solid Melts Into Air: The Experience of Modernity*, London, Verso.

BOURDIEU, P. and PASSERON, J-C. (1990) *Reproduction in Education, Society and Culture*, (translated by Richard Nice), London, Sage.

BRAUN, E. (1982) *The Director and the Stage: From Naturalism to Grotowski*, London, Methuen.

BRECHT, B. (1964) *Brecht on Theatre: The Development of an Aesthetic* (edited and translated by John Willett), New York, Hill and Wang.

BRECHT, B. (1965) *The Messingkauf Dialogues* (translated by John Willett), London, Methuen.

BROWN, R. (Ed.) (1973) *Knowledge, Education and Cultural Change*, London, Tavistock.

BRUNER, J. (1962) *On Knowing: Essays for the Left Hand*, Cambridge, MA, Harvard University Press.

COLLINGWOOD, R.G. (1958) *The Principles of Art*, Oxford, Oxford University Press.

DAVIS, D. and LAWRENCE, C. (Eds) (1986) *Gavin Bolton: Selected Writings*, London, Longman.

DEPARTMENT OF EDUCATION AND SCIENCE (1988) *National Curriculum: Task Group on Assessment and Testing Report (The TGAT Report)*, London, HMSO.

DEPARTMENT OF EDUCATION AND SCIENCE (1989a) *English for Ages 5 to 16 (The Cox Report)*, London, HMSO.

DEPARTMENT OF EDUCATION AND SCIENCE (1989b) *Drama from 5 to 16: HMI Curriculum Matters 17*, London, HMSO.

DEPARTMENT OF EDUCATION AND SCIENCE (1989c) *National Curriculum: From Policy to Practice*, London, HMSO.

DEPARTMENT OF EDUCATION AND SCIENCE (1990a) *English in the National Curriculum, (Statutory Order for English)*, London, HMSO.

DEPARTMENT OF EDUCATION AND SCIENCE (1990b) *Aspects of Primary Education: The Teaching and Learning of Drama*, London, HMSO.

DEPARTMENT OF EDUCATION AND SCIENCE (1991) *National Curriculum Music Working Group Interim Report*, London, HMSO.

DEPARTMENT OF EDUCATION AND SCIENCE (1991) *National Curriculum Physical Education Working Group Interim Report*, London, HMSO.

DODGSON, E. (1984) *Motherland*, London, Heinemann.

ECO, U. (1983) *The Name of the Rose* (translated by William Weaver), London, Secker and Warburg.

ESSLIN, M. (1987) *The Field of Drama*, London, Methuen.

FINLAY-JOHNSON, H. (1911) *The Dramatic Method of Teaching*, London, Nisbet.

FISCHER, E. (1963) *The Necessity of Art: A Marxist Approach*, Harmondsworth, Penguin Books.

FISKE, J. and HARTLEY, J. (1978) *Reading Television*, London, Methuen.

GEERTZ, C. (1973) *The Interpretation of Cultures*, New York, Basic Books.

GEERTZ, C. (1983) *Local Knowledge*, New York, Basic Books.

GOFFMAN, E. (1969) *The Presentation of Self in Everyday Life*, Harmondsworth, Penguin Books.

GREEN, M. (1970) *The Art of Coarse Acting*, London, Arrow Books.

GROTOWSKI, J. (1969) *Towards a Poor Theatre* (edited by Eugenio Barba), London, Methuen.

HAMMERSLEY, M. and HARGREAVES, A. (1983) *Curriculum Practice*, London, Falmer Press.

HARRIS, R. (1983) *Gotcha! The Media, the Government and the Falklands Crisis*, London, Faber and Faber.

HARRISON, T. (1985) *The Mysteries*, London, Faber and Faber.

HARVEY, D. (1989) *The Condition of Postmodernity*, Oxford, Basil Blackwell.

HOBSBAWN, E. and RANGER, T. (Eds) (1983) *The Invention of Tradition*, Cambridge, England, Cambridge University Press.

HOLDERNESS, G. (1988) *The Shakespeare Myth*, Manchester, Manchester University Press.

HORNBROOK, D. (1989) *Education and Dramatic Art*, Oxford, Basil Blackwell.

KEMPE, A. (1988) *Drama Sampler*, Oxford, Basil Blackwell.

KEMPE, A. (1990) *The GCSE Drama Coursebook*, Oxford, Basil Blackwell.

LARKIN, P. (1988) *Philip Larkin: Collected Poems* (edited by Anthony Thwaite), London, Faber and Faber

LAWTON, D. and CHITTY, C. (Eds) (1990) *The National Curriculum*, London, Institute of Education.

LÉVI-STRAUSS, C. (1964) *Structural Anthropology*, Harmondsworth, Allen Lane The Penguin Press.

MAYAKOVSKY, V. (1970) *How are Verses Made?* London, Jonathan Cape.

MILLER, J. (1986) *Subsequent Performances*, London, Faber and Faber.

MORTON, D. (1989) *Assessment in Drama: Discussion and Working Document*, City of Leeds Department of Education.

MYERSCOUGH, J. (1988) *The Economic Importance of the Arts in Britain*, Policy Studies Institute.

NATIONAL CURRICULUM COUNCIL (1990a) *English: Non-Statutory Guidance*.

NATIONAL CURRICULUM COUNCIL (Arts in Schools Project) (1990b) *The Arts 5–16: A Curriculum Framework*, Harlow, Oliver and Boyd.

NATIONAL CURRICULUM COUNCIL (Arts in Schools Project) (1990c) *The Arts 5–16: Project Pack*, Harlow, Oliver and Boyd.

O'NEILL, C. and LAMBERT, A. (1982) *Drama Structures*, London, Hutchinson.

PAVIS, P. (1982) *Languages of the Stage: Essays in the Semiology of the Theatre*, New York, Performing Arts Journal Publications.

REA, K. (1989) *A Better Direction*, London, Calouste Gulbenkian.

RICOEUR, P. (1981) *Hermeneutics and the Human Sciences* (edited and translated by John B. Thompson), Cambridge, England, Cambridge University Press.

RODGERS, P. (1989) *The Work of Art: A Summary of the Economic Importance of the Arts in Britain*, London, Calouste Gulbenkian and Policy Studies Institute.

ROUSSEAU, J-J. (1960) *Politics and the Arts: The Letter to M. d'Alembert on the Theatre* (translated by Allan Bloom), Glencoe, IL, Free Press.

ROWELL, G. (1971) *Victorian Dramatic Criticism*, London, Methuen.

SLADE, P. (1954) *Child Drama*, University of London Press.

SLADE, P. (1958) *An Introduction to Child Drama*, London, Hodder and Stoughton.

TAYLOR, R. (1986) *Educating for Art*, London, Longman.

WATKINS, B. (1981) *Drama and Education*, London, Batsford.

WATSON, R. (1990) *Film and Television in Education*, London, Falmer Press.

WAY, B. (1967) *Development through Drama*, London, Longman.

WERTENBAKER, T. (1988) *Our Country's Good*, London, Methuen.

WILLIAMS, R. (1961) *Culture and Society, 1780–1950*, Harmondsworth, Penguin Books.

WILLIAMS, R. (1977) *Marxism and Literature*, Oxford, Oxford University Press.

WILLIAMS, R. (1988) *Resources of Hope*, London, Verso.

WILLIS, P. (1990) *Common Culture*, Milton Keynes, Open University Press.

WITKIN, R. (1974) *The Intelligence of Feeling*, London, Heinemann.

WITTGENSTEIN, L. (1980) *Culture and Value*, (edited by G.H. von Wright and translated by Peter Winch), Oxford, Basil Blackwell.

WOLFF, J. (1981) *The Social Production of Art*, London, Macmillan.

YOUNG, M. (Ed.) (1971) *Knowledge and Control*, London, Collier-Macmillan.

Index

Abbs, Peter, *xi*, 2
acculturation, 109
achievement, 70, 72, 78, 91,
    104, 125–128, 131, 139–140,
    157, 162
acting, 4, 8, 24, 72, 101, 119,
    129, 134
acting out, 8
actor, *ix*, 1, 3–4, 6, 23, 27, 31,
    45–46, 48–50, 52, 56–57,
    59, 62–64, 70, 77, 81–83,
    86, 89, 96, 98, 104–105,
    107–109, 126, 129, 137–138,
    151, 158
    holy, 25
actor's performance, 83, 104,
    106, 116
administration, 6, 83, 151
advertising, 77, 87
Aeschylus, 31
aesthetic, 19, 20, 33, 36
    education, 36
    field, *ix*, 18, 20
    grounded, 33–34, 37
    knowledge, 112
    personal, 20

principles, 104
recognition, 36, 38, 41, 121
theory, 19, 24
agit-prop, 53
A-level, 6, 16
alienation techniques, 144
allegory, 144
ambiguity, 144
*Amédée, or How to Get Rid of
It*, 106
anti-intellectualism, *ix*
appraising, 111, 128, 160
aptitudes, 6, 128, 131
art, 20–25, 29–37, 39–40,
    70–71, 78, 112–113
    as a cultural system, 38
    child, 18
    form, 11, 19
    process, 20
    pseudo-, 34
    visual, *x*, 1, 11, 14, 70, 72,
        80, 84, 88, 111–112,
        127–128, 139, 162
    -works, 21
Artaud, Antonin, 24, 25
artistic faculty, 20

90, 101, 111, 113–114,
128–129, 131, 156
curriculum, 2–7, 12–14, 36,
38, 54, 58–59, 68, 71–72,
88, 110, 112, 129–130,
133–134, 136, 137,
139–140, 156–157
experiments, 90
form, 133–134
knowledge, 129
literature, 137
metaphor, 40
pedagogy, 13, 68
performance, 13, 53, 56, 105
play, 136, 141, 148
product, 69–71
signifiers, 109
spectacle, 47
techniques, 132
text, 50, 52–53, 58, 112,
134–135, 156
vocabulary, 115, 136
dramatised society, 56
dénouement, 144

East Enders, 48
Easter Island, 40
editing, 55, 57, 79–81, 88, 143
educational drama, 8
education in drama, 2, 10, 22,
36, 57, 59–60, 62, 64, 88,
112, 114, 130, 137, 156, 158
Education Reform Act, 1988,
7, 11–12, 14, 156, 157
effects, 85, 101, 106–107, 144
Elizabethan period, 138
English, 1–2, 5, 7, 9–10, 14,
16, 19, 97, 112–113, 117,

125, 127, 132–133, 136, 138
Working Group, 9–10, 125
entertainment, 44, 98
entitlement, 2, 157
Esslin, Martin, 12
Eucharist, the, 27
Eumenides, The, 31
European,
history, 30
society, 30
theatre, 24, 99
tradition, 138
evaluating, 111
examination
boards, 110, 126
practicals, 4, 48
expectations, low, 82
experimental, 89
experimenting, 75, 88, 120,
134
exploration, 88
exposition, 144

Falklands War, 64
Fanshen, 114
farce, 136
Fawlty, Basil, 56, 98
Festival of Remembrance, the
annual, 47
film making, 50, 73, 79
films, 6, 54, 79, 95, 106
Finlay-Johnson, Harriet, 68
Fischer, Ernst, 113
flash-back, 122, 143
fly-men and women, 52
form, 2, 89, 97, 113–114, 136,
149
frame, 98–99, 122
frame, spatial, 99